This is a first edition published by Press On Endeavors, Perterborough, Ontario

Printed and bound in Canada by Transcontinental

Cover and layout design by Robert W. (Robbie) Preston

See Index of Illustrations and Photographs

LIBRARY AND ARCHIVES CANADA CATALOGUING IN PUBLICATION DATA

Preston, Robert W., 1938-

The Canadian Empress : building the last Canadian cruise ship / Robert W. Preston.

Includes index.
ISBN 0-9737176-0-2

**1. Canadian Empress (Ship)--History. 2. Cruise ships--Ontario--Kingston--History.
I. Title. II. Title: Building the last Canadian cruise ship. III. Title:
Last Canadian cruise ship.**

VM461.5.C36P73 2005   386'.22436'097137   C2004-907296-X

Building the

LAST CANADIAN CRUISE SHIP

This is a story of how and why there is a
vessel called the **M. V. Canadian Empress.**

It is also the story of how and why I built the model of the vessel and some of the
many, many joys of working with and for Bob Clark as one of the builders of his
dream as well as one who got to sail a dream as its First Officer, the Mate.

This book is dedicated to my unseen grandchildren who someday will learn something
of their grandfather and his love of ships of all sizes and types.

It is also for Bernice J. (Lloyd) Preston, my Mother, who, as a little girl was raised
on the decks of the Great Lakes Schooner *Katie Eccles* sailing from the home port of
Napanee, Ontario.

As well as for her Mother, Mary Lloyd, who was the cook aboard the *Katie Eccles*
when it wrecked during the November, 22, 1922 storms against the Brother Islands in
Lake Ontario.

In my mind are their stories of life on a ship.

Building the

LAST CANADIAN CRUISE SHIP

All things created are works of love, for you have to have feeling for your subject. But it is your friend's love for you and/or your work at hand that gets the project finished into a book for others to enjoy as well.

My friendship list includes,

Elizebeth Ross, who helped by always asking how is the book coming?

Linda Hayes who used her heart and pencil with great skill.

James W. Demers, the author, who saw something in my book and asked me to finish it, so that he could do the first reading.

Lynne Frape-Trotter and Nancy Frey who did the final edit.

Also there are other friends who asked their names not be used here for they wish no credit for their ongoing help and support.

God bless and thank you one and all.   Robbie   July, 2004

Building the

LAST CANADIAN CRUISE SHIP

SOME AREAS OF THE SHIP
THAT MOST PEOPLE DON'T SEE

UNDER WAY AT LAST

NOTHING
IS IMPOSSIBLE

THE DREAMERS
AND
THE DREAM

THE HOME PORT

Kingston, Ontario is the home port of the ***Canadian Empress*** cruise ship. It is her home port of register, and it is also her port of layover for the winter months. She shares this port with some other very famous ships of the past that also called Kingston their home port at one time.

When our first prime minister, Sir John A. Macdonald, laid the cornerstone at the former Kingston Shipyards, on Ontario Street in Kingston, he opened the first drydock on the Great Lakes.

That drydock and site is now home to the Marine Museum of the Great Lakes and it holds a lot of the historical artifacts and recorded history of our maritime past in Canada.

Even before that event, boat building was a way of life along the shores around Kingston. Bateaux and Durham boats, at one time, had been and were the main means of travel on the water routes.

Bateaux in their prime time, were 30 to 40 feet in length. Those with 4 foot high hulls could carry 4 to 10 tons of people and freight. The bigger Durham boats could carry up to 10 times more freight with their lengths of 80 to 90 feet and beams of 10 feet.

The War of 1812 saw the creation of the first major Canadian ship on the Great Lakes.

There were many smaller vessels of various types of hull and sail configuration that took advantage of the wind in their sails but not of her type or size.

George Heriot reports in his travels (1807) that, "Vessels from fifty to a thousand tons burden were constructed at Kingston".

The *HMCS St. Lawrence*, as it was called, was a ship of the line, a man-of-war. It was 190 feet in length, a 3-decker, with 112 guns and carried over 1000 men and troops with a displacement of 2304 tons.

The *HMCS St. Lawrence* was built in Kingston on the grounds where the present Royal Military College stands, the site of the former Naval Yards of Upper Canada. For many years *HMCS St. Lawrence* held the record as the largest ship of any type on the Great Lakes and was also the largest warship of the British Navy anywhere, even larger than Nelson's *Victory.* The *HMS Victory* had only 110 guns.

More history was created and recorded about 20 miles west of Kingston, at Bath, Ontario. Just west of this small town, on the north shore of the Adolphus Reach, is the site of the former shipworks that created the *Frontenac.* This ship was created just after the war of 1812, in 1815-16. Most important this was the first North American-built ship on the Great Lakes to have steam power.

The *Frontenac* was a ship of massive size. A length of 170 feet, with a beam of 32 feet, and a weight of 700 tons made her a big vessel. The two paddle wheels were 40 feet in circumference and would push the ship along at about 10 knots. They were driven by a 50 hp steam engine. No longer did travelers or sailors need the wind to move them about the waterways. The *Queen Charlotte*

soon followed from the same yard in 1818.

So, what created all this shipbuilding activity over so many years in the Kingston Area? History records that more and more people had immigrated to Canada with all their worldly goods. The population explosion in Upper Canada by those here already increased the need for more goods from their home lands.

The East and West trade of goods and the movement of people increased daily in Canada. This created the need for more ships. Roads, as we know them, were still a dream in the minds of many. Most were footpaths or rough trails.

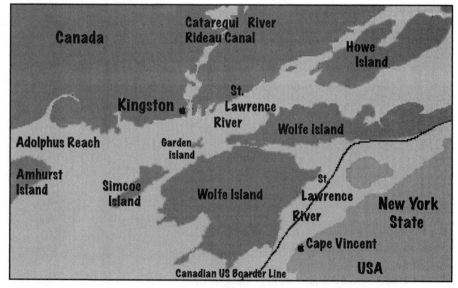

Map of Kingston area

Looking at the map, we have a better understanding of the Kingston area. The waters of the Cataraqui River/Rideau Canal system, flow into Kingston harbor from the north.

The west side of the harbor is washed by the waters of Adolphus Reach and Lake Ontario, the latter being the easternmost lake of the five Great Lakes of North America. Then we see that the whole of Kingston harbor fronts on the western end of that great river, the St. Lawrence.

This river, starting at Kingston, is one of the longest marine highways in the world for it goes some 900 miles from Kingston all the way to the Atlantic Ocean. Next, let your eyes scan down the map. After they drift over the famous Islands called Garden, Simcoe, and Wolfe you find the lands of New York State. This is a northern part of United States.

These different areas were all major players in the history of the western flow of people and goods to and from the centre of North America.

Garden, Simcoe and Wolfe Islands were the famous staging points for goods to the old world such as our great white pine and oak timber for ship building used in England. Much of Ontario's tall pine forests were stripped nude to fill the needs. When one looks at the flat rock area of Garden Island it is hard to think that more then fifty ships were built there.

Over time, the rivers soon became the major route for moving people and goods.

The St. Lawrence, like any other route, has its intersections. Intersections in all forms of life are where one will find development and growth whether it be good or bad.

Kingston, which became our nation's first capital, is at one of those major intersection along the St. Lawrence. People and goods were moved through, stopped at or, in a lot of cases, just plain started from this area. Fort Frontenac was built here long before a city was formed.

Before the tarmac highways of today, people and goods were moved by water vessels of many different types, following the shores of the rivers and lakes.

As the marine traffic increased, so did the size of these boats and some became ships. Soon we saw the passenger boats evolve from paddle and oar power to sail and then finally steam power. Today the props are turned by power from diesel engines.

The Great Lakes enjoyed the bigger vessels. With growth they ran regular routes and had a posted schedule for departures and planned arrivals.

Some Lakers were just like the riverboats in shape and style for they operated on the rivers and on the lake as well, and carried on the same type of trade. The

Lakers were just larger in size.

Life was simpler then. Delivery tomorrow, next week or even next month was very fast freight service. People were not yet driven by instant everything. But times changed as people obtained better vessels and a delivery promise date could be kept.

Canadian boats and ships came, over the years, to number in the hundreds. The tallies of 1835 show about 800 Durham boats in use and about 1,500 Bateaux working the St. Lawrence River above Montréal right up into Lake Ontario. 1863 tallies showed changes as the sailing vessels replaced them. Inventories showed 1,040 schooners and over 330 sailing vessels of other classes. Steamboats by then counted over 390 in number. Their numbers may have been smaller but their sizes were larger.

A captain would acquire a small vessel, and go into business with his own family as crew or hire a few friends. Some even built their own vessels. If they owned a farm, then they would build their vessel on the shore. Others used land at the edge of town. Some of these operations turned into ongoing ventures creating several vessels.

This need of service, travel, and the following prosperity, resulted in the growth of the great companies that created the ships that plied the St. Lawrence and the Great Lakes with stops in all sorts of ports.

Some ports of call were no more than a dock on the waterfront of a farm that the locals all used. In time these places became major ports of call.

The rivers made for some very special types of ships and boats. We even had those that ran the rapids down to Montréal and came back by the old Lachine Canal. Others had to fit the narrow channels of the islands or the box shapes of the locks. Depending on who you talk with, passenger ships were most abundant anytime between 1816 and 1949. Some will say the shipping lasted until 1965. This feeling depends on the lake or river system in question.

The Second World War also helped change a lot of things. In the years following the war, buses improved with stronger engines and more comfort built in for the longer trips. The diesel engine gave the buses and trucks a greater capacity for heavier loads, greater distance, higher speed, and faster profits with less government regulation than ships and shipping required.

People enjoyed their trips and holidays on the ships but it took one event to change it all. A small fire that got out of control on a ship while in port changed things forever.

The events of 1949 and shortly thereafter sounded the death knell for passenger ships sailing under the Canadian flag on the rivers and lakes of Canada and around the world.

The S. S. Noronic, was a Great Lakes steamer. It had been built at Port Arthur, (now called Thunder Bay)

Ontario in 1913 for the Northern Navigation Company. The vessel was later bought by the Canadian Steamship Lines to join its Great Lakes passenger fleet.

On the evening of September 17, 1949, while docked in Toronto harbor, and loaded with American passengers, the ship was consumed by fire. This tragedy caused 118 lives to be lost. Authorities claim the fire was of a spontaneous combustion nature, starting in a companionway closet.

The accident investigation exposed a lot of simple things that went wrong on board that night and cost a lot of people their lives. This sad event started a historical change of ships under the Canadian flag, and eventually the demise of the passenger ship business.

When all was said and done, it also was one of the major reasons Canada created some of the toughest marine standards in the world. These standards changed the rules for construction, training and the manning of ships of all types that sail under the Canadian flag. It now gives us the safety afloat we take for granted, to avoid that 1949 disaster happening again on any ship sailing under a Canadian Flag.

Every stage in the life of a ship is tightly inspected on a regular program. Each year in the spring, the crews of ships are tested and certified to perform their required job safely, with skill and understanding. The ships and all of their equipment are also inspected and tested.

Within a year or two of that disaster a large percentage of Canadian passenger ships were laid up for good. There were many reasons for this but fire, safety and training were the main ones.

When I was a kid, I would bike down to the Kingston waterfront and look at all the old passenger ships that lined the docks rotting from lack of use—dying ahead of their time. The great names were emblazoned in red, black or gold lettering on the sides of the bow and across the sterns with their home ports of call underneath.

In the staterooms of the *Canadian Empress* you will find prints from the N. A. Patterson photo collection that show some of the grand ships like the *Rideau King, Rapid Prince, Kingston, and Toronto*, just to name a few.

Most companies could not meet the upgrades needed to comply with the newer safety standards and the owners could not justify the cost of refits or even the cost of building new ships to replace the old vessels. They could not foresee a good return on their money.

The world had changed and was now changing even faster. Old was out, new was in and shipbuilding in Canada dried up as the market died or just changed to meet the new lifestyles we all enjoyed after the Second World War and the Korean War.

Remember how the TV changed your family's lifestyle? We used ships a lot less to move people and goods in Canada unless the cargo was going overseas like the billion of tons of Canadian grains each year.

The opening of the St. Lawrence Seaway in 1959 further changed the use of ships under the Canadian flag. We moved a lot of coal and iron ore in the new Seaway but not the travelers.

Nowadays, we use ships and boats mainly for something to do, recreation, a means to pass the time away, to relax and to enjoy life once again.

With all this relaxing during the summer, we see on an average day, 3,000 to 5,000 people taking day tour trips throughout the Thousand Islands system from both sides of the river and from several different ports of call along the great river called the St. Lawrence.

People come from all over the world just to see the famous Thousand Islands, which many claim were created by Paul Bunyan. The stories claim when Manitou, the Indian God, did not pay Paul for his work of digging the big ditch that Paul got angry. To get even, Paul tossed back piles of dirt in the ditch. Before Paul could fill in the big ditch completely, Manitou is said to have paid his bill. No one else would dig it out again. That is how we got all those islands and strange names in a funny pattern on the river.

Some visitors come for the other great stories of river life and folklore or to walk the castles or museums. Some come to see and study up close the stately homes of the rich and famous in the island area, others, just to be on the seaway; to watch the ocean ships go by; to see their chipped, rusted hulls up close; to feel and hear the deep, guttural vibrations of propellers. But when least expected, to some, the mighty blast of the steam whistle of a big salty makes their day.

Some ships' whistles, screech or roar or just blast sounds that pierce your ears and rattle your teeth as they sound their call for the right of way on the narrow river channels. Others sound warmly, blowing a friendly hello to fellow water travelers.

The St. Lawrence River Seaway system gives the ships connection to Thunder Bay, on the north west shore of Lake Superior. The 750 foot ships of the world, can travel around 2,400 miles inland to mid North America from the Atlantic Ocean, past Anticosti Island in the mouth of the St. Lawrence River, all the way up into the five Great Lakes of North America.

DAY DREAMERS

They are
the most dangerous people in the world.

For, not only do they dream of creating
or
doing things differently,
they are the ones who responded to
their visions.

They created all things good and bad
that make our world as we see it.

Robbie Preston

With all this recreation going on, in the new age, it gave a local Kingston day dreamer a good reason to dream out loud with his friends.

He is one of those people who lives at a place called Treasure Island. The Treasure Island of this story is downriver about 7 miles east of Kingston, on the north western edge of the Thousand Islands.

Treasure Island is no longer an island for it is connected to the mainland via a low causeway. It lies off the north shore, right beside the western end of the Bateaux Channel just up stream from Howes Island. Here the Bateaux Channel blends in with the Canadian channel, which is the river's main route up to Kingston.

This picture of him in joy was taken about an hour after the **Canadian Empress** was safely afloat on her own bottom.

The story that follows will help explain the many causes for his elated joy, satisfaction and pride that day as he made more history.

Mr. Robert (Bob) Clark was that day dreamer.

Bob Clark, the day dreamer, has been very active over the years with a few other great events in his area of the world.

Worthington Park, which is situated in North Kingston, is one of his many dreams come true. He is the creator and owner of Kingston's Premier mobile home park. What makes this mobile home park special was and is his high standards of the park in all matters. This image has earned it a five star rating in the mobile home parks industry in Canada. In 1981 only four other such parks held that high a rating in the whole nation.

In Confederation Park, across the docks from where the **Canadian Empress** ties up on her turn-around stop on the Kingston waterfront, sits the old stone building of the former Canadian Pacific Railway Station that is used nowadays by the local Chamber of Commerce for its tourist information centre.

Outside, on a section of the old Canadian Pacific Railway track bed, is parked one of Bob's other dreams. The "Sprit of Sir John A."

He was instrumental in it being placed there to help celebrate the first one hundred years of Canada.

You are reading about another of his many day dreams that came true. This book will detail one of "his" dreams that bore fruit, blossomed and became a love boat to many a traveler around the world.

The Spirit of Sir John A. (train)

SO,

WHAT DOES THIS ALL HAVE
TO DO WITH THE CANADIAN EMPRESS?

The *Canadian Empress* became a reality because of one of Bob's day dreams. It happened over a beer with friends one day. During the talk about things on the river that river people do, the increased volume of tourist traffic surfaced again like always. They talked of all things past and present, life on the river, of the latest changes as they could see them, how it felt to them, and the effect on their social life.

What surfaced and came to light was that there were no longer Canadian passenger ships on the river that people could stay on overnight, and really tour and enjoy all the islands like in the good old days.

They talked of when people travelled up the Rideau to Ottawa or down the St. Lawrence to Montréal. They even talked of what it may have been like in the good old days as the ladies sat topside and sipped tea, and the men with cigars played cards below to pass the time of the voyage.

They talked of real passenger ships that catered to the passengers' requests for fancy meals and ballrooms, unlike those 500-seat floating buses you see today that wander around some of the islands selling pop, hot dogs and rolls of film.

What sparked the talk that day was the passing downbound of The New Shorm, a small scale American cruise ship from Connecticut on its way to Québec.

This ship made a few trips each year from its starting point in Connecticut on the Atlantic seaboard, up the Hudson, through the Erie Canal to Lake Ontario at Oswego, down the Seaway to tour the Saguenay River in Québec, then back to Québec City where their trip would end.

A new voyage would start as the ship retraced its route back to Connecticut with a new group of bused-in passengers from the United States. People could not join the ship at a Canadian port. So much for the protection of Canadian business that did not exist.

That beer that day and a few little rums later turned 'why nots' and 'what-ifs', into a ship line that is known by many around the world. It was the seed that created "Rideau - St. Lawrence Cruise Ships". In the mid 80's, the name was later changed as we see it today to "St. Lawrence Cruise Lines Inc."

The *Canadian Empress* is the ship that is credited with reopening to the world the joy of river cruising in Canada onboard a ship sailing under Canadian flag and ownership.

The last few years we have even seen a major return to cruising ships on the Great Lakes by others ship operators who sail from both Canadian and American ports.

Bob Clark is known for covering the details, and has proven to be a great planner. It took a year and some to turn that dream of Bob's into lists of solid facts and action. He even confirmed what the government employees never knew for sure. He toured the Rideau Canal system himself, via yacht and on land, to confirm the trip would be enjoyable for passengers on a cruise.

Come winter, he was found back in the drained canal locks, making more notes and confirming measurements. Next was the money hurdle. Even with his past successes and business connections, it took time to raise the needed money of $1,700,000.00 to build the ship of

his dreams. But the government and others saw the light for this new type of tourist venture and helped him with low cost loans. It's amazing how people's minds had changed after 30 years.

There was the odd passenger or cruise ship sailing under a Canadian flag in those last thirty years. The *Selkirk Settler* built in the 1960's was operating on Lake Winnipeg. But a Canadian flag had not been raised on any new cruise or passenger ship that had been constructed in the past 20 years in Canada that would sail regularly in Canadian and American waters.

Cruising, which had fallen from the Canadians lifestyle and wants, was coming full circle again.

THE SHIP

THE SHIP

Bob Clark is a proud Canadian and a determined one. He would have his new Canadian-designed and built, calm-water, river-cruising ship that would be called *Canadian Empress*—something right out of the past.

German and Milne Inc. marine architects of Montréal were employed to be the designers of Bob's dream ship. For them was the task of transforming his dreams, his ideas, and his collected information into a vessel to accomplish his wishes. The results produced a ship to match Bob's greatest visions.

It was not to be any 'love boat', that was for sure, but a lot of people over the years have fallen in love with it.

About 40,000 people worldwide have enjoyed trips aboard the vessel since its maiden voyage in September of 1981. Many have returned over the years. For some their sailings aboard number over a hundred different voyages. Such response confirms Bob's day dreams were once again, good day dreams.

German and Milne Inc. have created a large number of great ships of all classes from little tugs to world class vessels, even Artic Ocean-going icebreakers. Their design number for *Canadian Empress* is #1142, which said a lot for their expertise. Each number is a notch on their drawing boards of one more successful vessel.

Even with this interesting and diverse background of vessels of many shapes and planned end-uses, the *Canadian Empress* was one of their toughest design jobs up to that time. They claim they had never had to design a ship of any type that had to fit in a box and/or fit that box as tight as the *Canadian Empress* had to and still function as planned.

So what was the size of this all-important box?

15

The magic box was the end result of the smallest of three major measurements of the many locks that make up the Rideau Canal system that flows uphill from Kingston to Smiths Falls, and then downhill to Ottawa. This was to be a major route of travel for the ship and it had to fit and work. Those limits were to set the measurements for draft, beam, length, and even the height.

Bob's own personally-obtained facts showed that the locks' minimums were 5 feet 6 inches deep (water over the sills), 32 feet wide, and 112 feet between the gates. The dream ship would later be built, with a draft of 4 feet 9 inches a beam of 30 feet and the length overall of 108 feet. Also, the ship had to be able to be reduced to a floating height overall of 22 feet to clear a few low bridges up the Rideau.

German and Milne Inc.'s major task was to create a cruise ship to suit Bob's notes and dreams. The ship on the outside was required to look like something old that could have sailed on the St Lawrence or the Rideau River, eighty to a hundred years before.

The magic box ruled out all those ideas that resembled those beautiful side or stern paddle wheelers. Side or stern paddle wheelers were too long or too wide and they wasted too much room in the box with a lot of lost revenue space on board.

So, they sharpened their pencils and worked on a shape that combined features of those long steam driven vessels with their big smoke stacks, even to their whistles that tell the nautical world of their navigational plans.

Now the designers showed their expertise, properly fitting all the various sizes of items that make up a ship. When you look at a cruise ship you are actually looking at a floating hotel. First, you have to have a hotel office and front desk. This is a good place for the purser to hide as he keeps track of all the ship's accounting and onboard business functions. Next, you need staterooms with sleeping berths, in order to make it pay.

The *Canadian Empress* had to contain the largest number of berths possible while offering some variations in quality levels, since it would not be carrying freight for extra profit like those old ships did.

She was fitted with 32 staterooms that sleep 66 passengers, plus the accommodations for crew. The vessel was also licensed to carry 120 passengers for day trips.

Even though the firm's minimum age for a passenger is fourteen, by Canadian marine law the ship is required to carry 10% of her total life jackets in a size to fit children. A strange law to some at times but I remember the time there was a need to switch to a smaller sized life jacket, in staterooms, for someone of small stature.

The design crew had to re-sharpen their pencils many, many times in order to squeeze and change the drawings and balance things as the ship also had to contain a meeting area for meals, entertainment, and a place to sit around if the weather did not suit the passengers for going topside or up to the foredeck to see where they were bound.

All ship's passengers always require food. Some would list the bar at the top of the list, but all travelers get hungry sooner or later with or without a bar. There also had to be a place to prepare light meals for passengers and crew. The idea was to serve the passengers a breakfast and a light lunch onboard as the ship cruised and stopped for shore tours. After the passengers had enjoyed their meals then the crew meals were readied. The evening or main meal of the day would be taken on shore, after the ship tied up each evening. It was believed that the galley was just too small to prepare major culinary delights for the passengers. Besides, each port of call had one or more of the many different restaurants that made the river ports famous for their eateries.

Some eateries are historical in nature, such as the Inn in Upper Canada Village. Here the passengers travel by horse and buggy through the park from the marina dock to the village to enjoy a meal in the old tavern. They were to be fed in a style and of similar fare enjoyed by stagecoach passengers of one hundred and fifty years ago.

The plans were that, after the shore suppers, the passengers would return for a delightful evening of on-board entertainment of different types, which would change nightly.

With these events, the Grand Saloon had to have its own sound system and entertainment centre and of course, there needed to be space for the bar, in this ever-changing multipurpose area.

Areas were required to hold the many different ingredients needed for the creation of the meals the chef was planning to serve.

Then there were also linens and towels needed for the Grand Saloon and for the staterooms. Linens require a clean, dry, secure place for storage and some place to store them after they are soiled and waiting to be taken ashore for cleaning.

Storage was also needed for all the different materials and equipment to clean the ship daily.

The problems were not over. As I mentioned, the ship is a floating hotel. They then had to juggle all the equipment and spaces that a ship of this type and size required to meet the ship building and safety laws and regulations for passenger ships sailing under the Canadian flag.

To meet the 'Safety of Life at Sea, International Convention', we see alarms bells, life jackets, life saving devices, sound systems, multi-purpose speakers, fire doors, fire hose and axes, water tight compartments, fireproof paints, finishes and very little wood.

Water is required for many purposes on a ship, from water mains for the fire stations to the water for sinks and showers in the rooms. The plumbing systems of the hot and cold water lines are looped so that when you open the hot water tap you waste very little water to get hot water. This system of hundreds of feet of pipes and fittings has to withstand the off-season sub-zero winter freeze ups. Then add thousands of feet of special wiring, emergency lighting, even air conditioning, piping and drains, not to mention the exhaust fans and vents to the outside from each shower.

For passenger safety there had to be potable water and holding tanks to contain the wastewater until it can be discharged ashore.

As with every floating hotel, it has to be moved daily, up and down the rivers to different ports of call.

Some things have to be fitted outside the hull. For greater control and smaller propeller size they elected to use twin propellers, a bow thruster and twin rudders that are all controlled from the bridge and wing area. Then there was the fitting of all the equipment in between that makes movement of the ship possible.

As you will later read, some controls are situated in several locations and are all interconnected.

THE WINNER IS...

As noted before, a lot of great ships have been built in the Kingston area in the past. Also, as noted below the first steamship was built just west of Kingston in Bath.

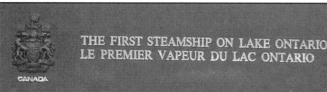

THE FIRST STEAMSHIP ON LAKE ONTARIO
LE PREMIER VAPEUR DU LAC ONTARIO

CANADA

In the early 1800's Kingston was a shipbuilding centre of note. The FRONTENAC, the first steamship to navigate Lake Ontario, was built here at Finkle's Point, Ernestown (now Bath), and launched September 7, 1816. Designed to carry freight and passengers, it was a boon to travellers, greatly reducing the difficulties and the cost of travel between Kingston and York (now Toronto). More sophisticated ships soon rendered the FRONTENAC obsolete and it was sold in 1825. Two years later it burned and sank in the Niagara River, but passenger steamships plied the lake for many years until rail and road travel became more effective.

The Frontnac launched Sept. 7, 1816,

The last was built just east of Kingston. Well, that's not really true. The *Canadian Empress* just looks like a steamship. She is really a diesel-powered vessel. So, for the true marine buff it is, *M.V. Canadian Empress*, not *S.S. Canadian Empress*.

The firm of Algan Ship Yard Inc., located in Gananoque, Ontario, 18 miles east of Kingston got the contract to build the ship. Gananoque, the river town of over 4,000 people in 1980, enjoys life at the confluence of the St. Lawrence and the Gananoque Rivers.

Algan Ship Yard Inc. was more known for its '500 seat, (bus type)' day tour boat construction than for building cruise ships. These are the tour boats which sail throughout the island tourist sites and are not of the cruise ship level of interior construction, furnishing nor details.

So it was interesting to find that Algan had the winning advantage over the Summer Town Boat Yard that is located down river near Cornwall.

A list would reveal reasons why

A.   They had a more central location closer to major suppliers in Kingston, Toronto, Montréal or Syracuse, NY for all things marine.

B.   Location for the ship's owner, Bob Clark, I think, was most important, for it was only about 8 or 9 miles from his home to the yard, by boat or car.

C.   Algan did have a track record for building vessels of this size. Their bus-type day tour boats are just a little bit larger than the *Canadian Empress*. And they too are built of Aluminum.

D.   Another feather in their cap was that they had just finished the *Lamer Law*, a vessel of 93 feet in length x 42 feet in beam, which was then, the largest all Aluminum Tri-hull sailing vessel in the world. This Canadian-owned dive-ship, which was built for the Cribbean dive-ship business, had garnered a lot of public attention. In the Caribbean, it would carry a 6-person crew and 18 guests. But that ship is another story for some other day.

E.   The *Canadian Empress* was to be built of aluminum as well, so they had the equipment and knowledge to undertake a project of this size. But on the other hand, they had never built a ship before of the magnitude of the *Canadian Empress*, as time would tell.

HULL # 45

The *Canadian Empress*'s keel was laid in November 1980 and was given a Canadian Coast Guard hull registration number V X 6 0 9 8.

For Algan, # 45 was their hull production number. It was a placard on a large sign that was mounted on the front of their building shed.

About two weeks after this event, Bob Clark commissioned me to build a scale model of the ship.

In conversation one day, Bob confessed he could not fully envision the transitions of the hull frame shapes in the area of the bow where the flat bottom plates rolled up to meet the vertical king post of the bow.

He located and tracked me down from an article that was in a local newspaper about my scale model building business. Bob was quite impressed with the overall detail of my work as he studied the photos of models I had created for others.

In time he learned that professional model building was just one of many trades that I enjoyed at that time in my life.

'Interesting,' is the best way to describe the events as we educated each other as to our forms of model building. Me, as to what I could do and how I would create models of different needs from scratch using full size drawing, some Plexiglass, other plastics, brass strips, with various types of glues, adhesives and paints, but very little wood. Bob Clark had been trying to create a model out of balsa wood but things were just not working. He soon learned from me why I had stopped building detailed ship models from wood. Wood is too alive and does strange things as it dries out or grows and cracks as the moisture level around it fluctuates.

Bob's basic problems were standard for most people in his position. First it was time consuming for him to learn how to correctly build a model to scale. Detailed scale model building is a real art form that not all can master.

Bob Clark was also busy with attending the shipyard every day, as well as keeping his hand into everything else in his very busy business life. The good lord only gives us 24 hours in a day and Bob used his entire quota plus a few extra.

After several coffees (no rums) we struck a deal. He decided that one of my models would also be good to have to help market the ship, since other people also had problems understanding his ship drawings and visualizing the true shape of the finished ship.

Very shortly that decision to order a professionally created model proved to be very important, in several different ways, for many different people.

The first brochures featured, on the front cover, a retouched photo of the ship's model.

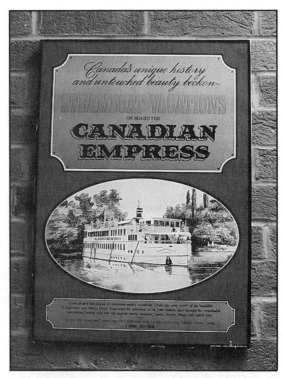

A plaque of the first brochures hanging outside the office

The creative photo work of B. Droppo

22

The etching of the vessel shown on the section pages and the cover of this book are of the same image that was created mechanically from a retouched photo of the ship's model that I had created back in 1980-81. This etching was created before the days of computer enhancement. On page 22, is one of the many staged shots. Kitchen plastic wrap made water with waves; angel hair made clouds and smoke from the stack; a photo drop out blue sheeting produced blue skys. Other secret tricks created the etched look and gave life to the pictures of the ship. The world saw not a picture of the ship under way on the river, but another view of a dream. The still waters of the island coves.

The building of the *Canadian Empress* scale model was to be a six-month contract for me for I had other work in my shop to complete ahead of Bob's time frame. But even the best laid plans of man and mice and river rats get changed.

January, 1981 was panic days for me and a few other people. With one phone call from Bob, everything changed. I was given the near-impossible task of less than ten days to finish the model. This was after having worked on the model for about 6 weeks of a 26-week delivery contract. Most of this time had been spent making my scale drawings and templates from a complete set of the ship drawings including all the latest changes.

The 10 days evolved into around-the-clock work, just like when we later built the ship. Only I did not have the noise or confusion of the other workers to contend with. It was just get up, grab something from the fridge, or build another peanut butter sandwich, make a big mug of coffee, head downstairs to the shop and build and build and build. It was non-stop work.

Time goes fast when you are having fun. Cool jazz is playing in the background. You're working in a profession you enjoy with deep passion. Even with Bob stopping by just to sit, to watch, to see the ever-changing shape, to empty an ash tray or just replenish the coffee mugs. It is amazing what a body can do. But round-the-clock brings total burn out. Non-stop shifts require sleep, at least in between them. Sometimes I stopped.

One time I was found sound asleep with a small part in my hand as I waited for the fast-drying paint to set.

Then came a final 31-hour non-stop stretch; a real non-stop adventure, which included presenting the almost finished model at the press conference. But I had created a model that was almost 95 % finished 5 months ahead of time. I got paints and glues and materials to do things that never worked before. I still am not sure how I did it. But that model still sits in Bob Clark's office.

We had a detailed scale model of 'the dream', a real *Canadian Empress*, a real ship at last, even if it was only built at a scale that was ¼ inch to the foot of the real full life size *Canadian Empress* being created on the building blocks in Gananque.

Appointments and detailing to the finished model were slightly different than what was in my mind when I started my creation but the end results served very well over the years.

What a proud moment I had on that first trip in May of 1982. It was a public relations trip, with media people onboard from all over the world. Crew training was over, the ship had just been christened, and I was on board to sail that trip as the new First Mate dressed in full double-breasted uniform with brass buttons, gold braid on the jacket arms and shirt epaulets. We did not yet have our officer's hats with all their scrambled eggs (see glossery) so I wore an Italian straw boater that I still own. It fitted right into place with the ship's image.

I had been introduced as the ship's First Mate, then reintroduced as the builder of the ship's scale model that sat on the bar for all to see and then reintroduced as a D of T, (see glossery) and a shipwright, who had worked on the construction of the ship itself, and the completion of some fine tunings to the vessel over the first winter.

WHY THE RUSH?

The panic, the rush, came from a last minute problem and a new dream.

Bob's Problem

It was a problem due to information that had surfaced. The business world rumbled of another Canadian organization that was planning to build a similar type of cruise ship. Studies showed there might not be a ready market for both concepts.

Bob's Latest Dream And Idea

To have the first press and media conference to give public exposure of the ship's concept, and of the tourist potential behind it, the **Canadian Empress** project would flower, bloom, for all to hear and see at the Holiday Inn in Kingston, in January, 1981. This was several months before the ship would be completed. World-wide exposure would also help with advance sales. Best of all it would start new dreams in many other people's heads of what a trip on the river would be like.

Like anything else in the media world, first blood got all the press love.

Bob Clark had done his homework very well for, all the right people were there, including me with the model. I was so tired that my wife did not even trust me to drive our car there that day.

My burning the midnight oil, those 10 days, put all the right polish on his dream.

I told you day dreamers are dangerous people. They can be hard on someone else's lifestyle for some-

The Star of the show

times their dreams can become infectious to others. It is not hard to see their dreams and the pleasure. Pain becomes something for tomorrow when there is more time for it to be a problem.

What a day! Even Bob Clark had tears in his eyes and bags under them too—just like mine. He was one of very few people who really knew what it took to put that model there. The end result was worth it for us both. The model of the **Canadian Empress** was the star of the show.

It took all the limelight, even made a small fortune for Kodak as press and other media reporters took pictures from every possible angle.

It was there in the centre of all things that day, a three-dimensional scaled vision that people could understand and relate to. Canada would have a new cruise ship with big red and white flag on its stern staff.

It completed the vision for people's minds of how the **Canadian Empress** would look. People could see the knife edge bow, the hard chine hull, the flat run of the tiller flats, the strutted shafts and wheels, (props) the offset rudders, even the thruster tunnel that runs athwart the ship's bow section with its prop in the middle of the tunnel. Right there on the bridge wings were the controls to put the ship alongside any sea wall.

The requirements were all there, the places to

sit, the railing for people to lean on as the ever-changing slide-show of the rivers flowed by.

With a drink in hand, the dreamed-of warm sun in their faces or the glow of moon and clouds lighting the river, making new memories, they could feel it all.

People heard the snicker of the sliding shuffleboard pucks and the click of the giant checkers during a game of shipboard life on the river. Big people with little kids' dreams could and would go fly a kite from the stern of the ship as they enjoyed the rivers in a new but old life style.

The model and the press release saved the day for everyone. People now dreamed of traveling on a real Canadian passenger ship again. They wanted to sail on the *Canadian Empress*; to wake up and see the mist on the river; feel the gentle, soothing movement of the ship at anchor in the islands; watch the clutch of ducks paddling nearby, as they too, started a new day of leisure.

In their minds they could feel the vibrations, the deep gutteral shrill of the steam whistle as it speaks of the Captain's directions of his planned action for the vessel, the reply whistle of a salty's deep mournful sound as it answers the call for safe right-of-away and passage up and down the channels of the seaway.

Nothing would compare to the dreams of many that afternoon.

Some tea in the Grand Saloon with its classic tin plate ceiling and the waitresses in their floor length skirts and white ruffled blouses, or ships officers in their double breasted uniforms with gold braid on their arms and hats. Such were the regal views-to-come for many.

The dreams were now exposed to all, in fact there was to be a reality to all this, the real ship was on the ways in Gananoque, completion due later in the summer of 1981.

River cruising was back in Canada. Sailing aboard a Canadian ship with a Canadian flag flying proudly from the stern mast.

MEANWHILE
BACK AT THE YARD

Work went on.

In the past the ships and boats of all types were made of local timber. Then we saw the change to iron hulls as the vessels got bigger; iron ships with thousands of rivets. At the same time, we saw the change from sail to steam, with paddle wheel and propeller driven vessls being created.

Later in time came the change to welded steel. This advancement made for even stronger and larger vessels. No matter what the hulls were made of, they all had the one common fault. They were always created or finished with a beautiful but hazardous material—wood. Wood could burn or, worse still, rot. Wood requires tender love and care all the time. Wood was used to finish the interior of ships and that always meant large amounts of paint and varnish.

If a fixture was built ashore in some fancy hotel you can rest assured that it was just as beautiful when done on a ship by the shipwrights of the past.

Times changed and so did the ships and how they were built and how they looked.

The *Canadian Empress* was to be truly a different ship in many ways. She would not be a steamship but she was created and built to resemble one with her big stack and quaint old looking shape. Her hull was not made of wood, iron or steel but was created from lightweight aluminum sheeting, a proven method of plate on frame welded construction shipbuilding.

She was to be truly a different vessel in many, many other ways. She started out being built upside down. The belly of the ship with the main keel and rib frames was laid out and built up on the builder's blocks, upside down.

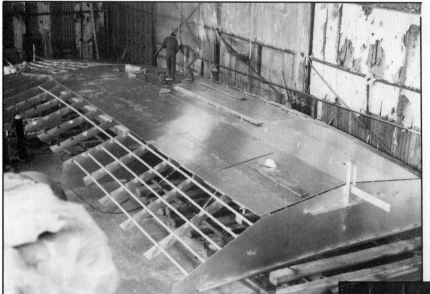

The lower hull section being built upside down

of the plates and outer seams as the welders worked on their hands and knees instead of laying on their backs and doing overhead welding. Even so, there would be some of the normal laying on their back under a ship and doing overhead welding. The hull's outer shell skin was plated with 5/16 inch aluminum sheeting and all the other plating thoughtout the ship was 1/4 inch thick aluminum plates and welded onto the aluminum frames of different thickness and bends as required in their different areas of use.

This reversal allowed the fitters, welders, and shipwrights to work faster and easier. The crews could walk among the frames on a flat surface as they aligned and jigged everything into place, waiting for the welding of the many joints, and the seams of the shell skins to be done.

The outer plates were just lowered into place rather than dragging the plates in under the frame skeleton and then pulling and/or lifting them tightly up to the frames for welding.

Another big advantage came from all the time saved with the speed of doing flat welding

The hull being lifted up on its side as part of the procedure to it being set on the building cribs

Having the Alcan Aluminum Plant a few miles away in Kingston was very helpful in the supply of all the aluminum stock sheets, plates, angle sizes and shapes required for the completion of the vessel.

A construction advantage of aluminum is that it can be worked with normal power tools used in the wood working industry.

Framing for the forepeak
The round holes are part of the thruster tunnel

With care and lubrication one can saw aluminum on a band saw, table saw, even use a router or jig saw. It drills easily if you use a wax lubricant on the cutting tips. But, remember Murphy and his Law. For those that don't know of Murphy's Law check in the glossary. Well, he played a big part in this ship.

Soon the collection of plates and frames started to take on the shape of a vessel. Like any major project of construction there are some stages of work advancement that mark a change in things.

For a ship of this type, one change that comes to mind is where you start to need a ladder to get into the different sections below the main deck as the bulkheads are fitted into place.

A ladder to the St. Lawrence Deck

Next, you find major changes are really visible they have dropped in place a piece of major equipment. As you walk along the cat walks or scaffolding you see the shafts in place, pumps fitted in the tanks and valves fitted to the pump and pipelines to control the flow of the liquids that will be held in those different tanks. Now they add the drive engines, transmissions, generators and transformers and all the electrical switching gear.

Soon there are plumbing pipes going everywhere and electrical wiring soon to follow.

Next, you find a flat deck under foot and man-holes cut in the decks with ladders sticking out of the holes that now lead below to the different tanks and compartments, as we call them, onboard.

At one point it just looks like any day tour boat with its big empty main deck—moreso when they closed in the deckhead of the main level.

The next big advancement to things was the aft part of the second deck. The Grand Saloon area had beautiful large window openings. The stern deck had the pillers to support the top deck and the low wall. It would be some time before the wooden handrail would be fitted.

Soon there were the stairs to the top deck from the stern deck and then at the bow there were those going from the bow deck up to the bridge walk-around.

As you cross the top deck you could now see and feel the thickness of the two strong backs that carry the expanse of the top deck and ceiling structure over the Grand Saloon.

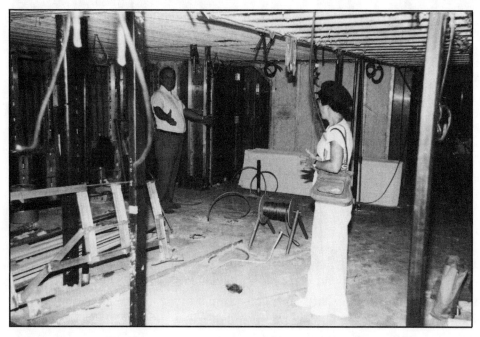

"This here is stateroom eight" gestures Bob Clark to a guest who is standing in the companion-way-to-be, outside of the area of state room 5.

MY
SECOND ENCOUNTER
WITH THE LADY

After returning mid-summer from a month-long motor-camping trip to the western United States, Mount St. Helens, Vancouver Island, plus a trip over the Canadian Rockies and back with my wife and a curious 10 year old son, the question was in the back of my mind, "How advanced were they in building the ship?" If I remembered right, it was to be ready for sea trials almost any day now.

So, one day, with equal curiosity, my wife and son joined me as we took a drive to Gananoque. We just had to see what had happen to the lady while we were gone.

We knew there would be changes, but our eyes got many surprises as we walked into the building shed that day.

Many weeks had passed since we three had last viewed the continual growth and changes in the ship. Its shape now filled the inside of the building shed.

My son Shawn could not believe that it was looking just like the model that I had built as we roamed in and out and over the top of the ship. He pointed out the different parts of the ship he had learned about from the drawing and model in my shop from the months before.

That drive to Gananoque was filled with more surprises for it changed a direction in the lives of we Prestons; in time, I would add another craft to my many others. Within the year I would complete my studies, obtain my license to become a ship's officer and work this ship as the Mate.

On the QT, I quickly learned things in general were behind schedule. Major ship building in the Kingston area had been a thing of the past for last twenty years. We learned that in a few weeks there was to be the planned launching on the first Saturday of September.

The date may be different but on page 19 you will notice that 165 years earlier was the launch of the *Frontenac* in Bath. History in the making.

The yard and Bob Clark needed people. That was for sure. But what they really needed was skilled tradespeople who knew what or how to work on a ship of this type or who could adapt their skills and other crafts to the needs at hand.

My years of working in the Kingston Ship Yard would once again put me in good stead. I had worked there as a fitter, lead hand, but also as a loftsman. These are the people who translate the drawings of a ship's design into the full size templates used to lay out, mark the material at hand and to make the parts of a ship.

Shipbuilders and shipwrights had become a truely rare breed of people in this part of central Canada. People, like myself, dropped out of the industry in the mid 60's when the work and the future of secure year round employment dried up for those in the repairing or building of ships. You were forced to relocate to the east or the west coast if you wished to enjoy that creative form of work, year round, in the boat/ship building business in Canada.

There was, at times, some work at Port Colburn Shipyards on Lake Erie or Collingwood Shipyards on Georgian Bay. But that life was not for me at that time.

I roamed the ship and took it all in. It brightened my memory of past working conditions from days long gone by in the old Kingston Shipyards, twenty years before.

What was incredible was to study the details of different parts of the ship that I had created in miniature scale a few months before. The yard had closely followed details, unlike any other ship.

Bob Clark spotted me as I wandered in and out of the compartments. It was not long before he cornered me and asked if I would come to work for him.

The truth was, I found out later on the return drive home, Bob had questioned my wife, and knew my model bench was empty of paying work, and my pockets as well, after the extended family vacation. He also knew from his visits to my model shop that I had shipbuilding experience, knowledge of the different jobs at hand and the skill for some of the jobs that he needed done. So, I went to work as a labourer. But that changed within the day. He soon found out and understood that I had been a loftsman, a combination fitter/welder in the old days. I was soon up to my ears using all my skills in the detail work of helping to finishing the vessel.

THE LAUNCH
OR
SHOULD WE SAY,
THE YANK

What fun a launch is! For the owner, his dreams get uncovered for all the world to see. He enjoys the limelight with his new ship, as the building shed calves its latest offspring.

For the yard it is a positive sign of another successful project when the hull is afloat. In the back of their minds is the age-old question, when do they start the next one?

What fun can a launch be for you the worker, you ask? For all the crew, who have no names now— the ones who pulled the long hard hours to make it all happen—it is their time to proudly stand on the sidelines with family, friends and fellow workers.

You will hear boastfully and boldly-made statements, "We did it." "Without us the damn thing would never float." Then you would hear a smart comment or two like the standard launching joke, "Did anyone close the sea chest valves?" "Who put the plug in?" "Hell, I bet you a five spot it won't even float."

All is in good fun for they, with everyone else, are proud to be a part of a new page in the marine history of Canada. At the time, one does not think of it as making history but every launch that takes place is a major turning point in marine travel and history on the river and Great Lakes.

I remember those days at the Kingston Ship Yard as a younger man. The vessels were launched abeam (side ways) into the water. A vessel was built on top of wooden cribs, much like the way the *Canadian Empress* was built.

At pre-launch time the vessel was lifted with rows of wooden wedges driven by the heavy blows of thirty or forty men swinging sledgehammers. Big clips on the side of the ship held heavy cables, which secured the vessel to the shore till launch time. Hammer blow after hammer blow still rings, in my ears. Teams of men would physically raise the vessel the extra height of an inch or two needed to lift the weight off the building cribs.

Before the launch the work was hard because the slide and batter boards that the ship would ride on to the water had to be set up under a vessel and cribbed into place. You dragged, pushed and pulled to get the log timber slides in under the vessel. Plus there were the hundreds of extra timbers to make the new cribs to mount all this new framework on.

Gallons of black tallow were slathered on the slide and batter boards which made a slippery sandwich to say the least. The batter boards with sloping slide plates on top were placed up under the ship. Then began the job of fitting new cribbing to support them on their correct slope. The black tallow would ooze out from between the joints as they took up the weight. The damn stuff would get on everything. But soon the vessel was ready for the void between the slide and the vessel was cribbed securely. The cribbing bore the weight of the mass as the finishing wedges were banged into place.

Now the vessel sat on two sets of cribs, the building cribs, and the launch cribs.

On launch day the safety cables were replaced with ropes, just before the big show. Under the drum-taut (see glossary) big manila ropes lay the chopping blocks with the sun dancing on the razor edges of the launchers' axes nearby.

On signal, the bang...bang...bang of the sledge hammers could be heard... and up rose the ship...only an inch or two. Shear human strength and old fashion manpower, lifted the vessel clear of the building cribs. Now the full weight of the ship sat on the slides. The ship was almost ready to make that slide onto the water.

With the weight off the building cribs that the ship was created on, came the job which saw the building cribs quickly dismantled and cleared for the safety of all nearby, and for the safe sliding of the ship as it travelled down to the water.

Extra tallow was coated on the ramp for it would melt with the shear heat of the sliding friction. No one ever wanted a hung vessel.

All would be ready. Workers combed their hair, brushed dirt from their faces, watched with pride and listened for the fanfair topside to cease and the speakers to complete their part of the launch show.

We stood silently and listened. From above we heard the 'Pop'! of that magic bottle of champagne cracking on the hull as the ship was given its name.

Those close by the ropes heard another sound.

Just a single plain, clear, " Whack!"

The pop of the bottle was the signal to chop the ropes and set the ship free to slide onto the water. The whack was the single sound of all the axes severing the ropes at each cutting station in a single unison blow.

The vessel picked up speed as it started its slide down the ways just from the shear weight and the angle of the slide ramps. Those close by could smell the stink of the hot tallow. With a big 'Plop', a 'Splash', it was afloat. The safety cables secured to the vessel held.

Not For The Canadian Empress

None of this for the **Canadian Empress.** It would be a different form of ship launching. A birthing to be remembered. Yes, very different and unplanned in some matters, that was for sure. This lady did not take lightly to the planned big push or to getting her bottom wet.

The **Canadian Empress** was built in a shed not out in an open yard. She had not even been rained on yet. She rested stern end to the water, not broadside to the water. She was built on top of the tracks of the marine railway, which ran right up into the building shed.

A house moving crew which had been contracted arrived and made ready the ship for her launch date. Algan being a small yard, never had a Millwrights' Shop, or a crew with training, whose job it would have been to ready the ship from her building blocks for her roll down the tracks into the water.

Instead of slide plates, batten boards and slimy black tallow, they installed the rail cars on the tracks under the ship to carry the load as it was readied for launching. They used jacks to lift the ship off its old cribbing and wedged it tight to the cribs on the rail cars.

The plan was to have the smiles, take the pictures, and endure the speakers.

Myrna and the Bottle

Everyone wanted Myrna Clark's job (She is Bob Clark's wife). Hers was a simple and easy but important job that day. She just had to give the vessel the name, then smack the champagne bottle on the hull. 'Pop'! goes the bottle with champagne bubbles floating everywhere. Someone else would chop the rope when they heard the pop, and down the track the **Canadian Empress** would roll and it would be afloat.

Like other things connected with the **Canadian Empress** this simple plan got changed. How many times have you dropped a bottle only to have it explode? Well, Myna Clark's face was one of suprise when the bottle in her hand bounced back at her. Yes, the bottle had been scored with a glass cutter to weaken it. No such luck. Alumimium is a solf metal that gives and flexes. So, Myna had to redo her little bit and put her all into it. The picture of her on page 37 tells the story.

Some More Of Murphy's Law, One Could Say.

The **Canadian Empress** is different in many ways; tall, straight vertical sides with no tumble home. and nice new special white marine fireproof paint on her full 30' wide beam.

Alongside the marine railway at water's edge was a tall wooden building that had been there for many years.

"Oh,........ oh," was the word when they opened the shed doors to the water and let the light shine on the snow-white mass of the fine lady's stern for the first time. When sighting down the ship's side, it was discovered that the building roof overhang could block the ship's passage to the water.

"No problem," said many. When the ship gets there it will just slide under it. The bets were soon laid down. Some people were going to win or lose money on this launch, that was for sure.

Act One

All the standard parts of any pre-launch finally happened. The great forgotten speeches were heard by all that listened. Myrna had completed her big, 'Whack'.

We can just cut it off

Act Two

The **Canadian Empress** added a new event. The ship was rolled out and down to the edge of the building—and stopped. It was obvious that it would not clear the roof overhang. That stop held her just short of her first collision with a land mass.

Act Three

Soon a crew with chainsaw climbed on board and used the top deck as a work platform from which they removed the corner of the roof's overhang from the old building.

Act Four

Now the fun was about to start again. Murphy was hiding around the corner laughing to himself over this new twist.

"Man can walk on water,
if he moves fast enough,
just don't stop"
Robbie Preston

Some people forgot the ground loading of all those extra weighty things that were on board the **Canadian Empress** at this time, as she was now sitting on those marine rail cars.

All the extra equipment was never a part of any other ship built in that shed, which made for a heavy load.

But, like any ground at waters edge, it can be soft or spongy—less supporting. So the track compressed into the ground as the ship stood still and waited for the chainsaw crew to do their thing. This dip in the track slope was not planned for. Therefore no equipment was

Help, I am stuck

They huffed and they puffed.

on hand powerful enough to pull the ship back up the track to get a good rolling speed again.

Pictured are two of the three large house moving winch trucks which tried. They managed to pull the lady up the track some. "Woah!" was heard. Now they found the track was bending out of shape. The word "stop!" was heard by many. The powers to be looked and pondered.

Act Five

After some time of studying the situation it was decided to let the ship roll free again. She rolled slow and then came to a stop. The **Canadian Empress** found a new dip in the track.

Remember I spoke of a ship being hung up on a launch. The danger was now clear. The vessel was only a little wet. It could not be pulled up the track due to the damage to the track. Now that it set in the wet it meant that divers would be needed to check the problem and make real sure the ship should, would, and could safely complete the launch.

After all was said and done it was decided that the launch was on hold till the next day.

Act Six

In the harbour that day, there was a small tug that had been working the area. Its captain had come into the small harbour at Gananoque to get a ringside water view

since it is not every day a new ship is launched. Little did the captain know, as he sipped his coffee, that soon he would be a hero for a day or so.

'Little toot' to the rescue one might say.
An answer to the problem at hand.

Like all true mariners, the good captain was willing to assist a ship in distress, which the **Canadian Empress** sure was at this time of her new life.

Act Seven

Sunday Sept. 6 we all gather again to wonder. Soon the tug got in position and lines and ropes were laid between the vessels to take the strain. A few more words were said. Then with a blast from the tug's whistle, a surge of churned-up water, and the slack was being taken up. All was ready.

Soon the water was a big mud puddle for hundreds of feet around. The tug's stern settled deeper down in the water as the captain added more and more power.   No luck as the lady had to weigh over two hundred tons. The captain called "all clear," for safety. With an eye on the ropes and an eye on the engine tachometer, he opened the throttles wide. Horns blew, whistles sounded.   With a yank from those extra revs we saw that energy translate into smooth rolling motion as the *Canadian Empress* moved out of its little depression in the rails.

Smoothly, like a lady, she rolled down the rails and slid gracefully to her rightful place in history. About 24 hours later then planned.

At last she floated on her bottom, as we of the sea would say. Which was great as no-one had any other idea of how to get her off the rail cars with out damage. Later it proved that the rail system required a lot of repairs.

The *Canadian Empress* set a new record for a rolling launch taking two days to complete such a short trip. The marine gods had really been looking out for the *Canadian Empress* on her launch days.

Now you understand why Bob Clark had a beer in hand and a super big grin on his face that day. History will tell more later on.

IN PUBLIC VIEW

The fanfare was over quickly and the drinks were enjoyed. It was a Kodak day, and weekend for all.

Now came the rush job of getting it finished and ready to do the job it was designed for. Each day the pressure had been increasing as another trip was cancelled. Bob Clark had lost about 4 weeks of revenue trips. The sailing season was fast coming to an end for 1981 just about as fast as Bob Clark's money chest was draining dry because of all the added expense from overtime hours for the many crew and workers plus the gallons of free coffee to his helping friends.

The ship was to be ready for shakedown by August and to start trips by September. Well, that part was history now. The beehive had had its little rest stop—longer than planned—but it had felt good to a tired body.

Things quickly fell back in place again as the power lines onboard were hooked up to shore connections to run all the tools and the lights. Like ants, there was now a steady stream of workers and others, of all size, shapes and dress going on board to start to work again.

The tons of material including the steel wall panels went up the gangways. All was piled ready for the next phase, the finishing and the detailing of the ship.

But now we were to complete things in the public view . The Algan Boat Yard was not like most other yards. The dock the *Canadian Empress* was tied to was open for all to see and approach. Now we had real fun. We worked, out in the open eye of the public, to finish all the appointments of the ship as she took on her finished look.

Some public came down to the harbor each day to sit in lawn chairs, across the street in the park, and watch the goings on. Others came to spot the latest changes and make their suggestions and ask their ten thousand questions. They would stop, buttonhole someone who would listen to them or when they spotted someone they knew.

Again, just like when I first joined the yard, many things were taking place all at once. Welders were working very hard at the slow process of welding thousands of feet of joints in the plates and welding plates to frames. Others were finishing the outer plate surface of the hull, grinding the welds smooth, and filling little voids to ready every thing for the hull painting.

Some jobs were held up just because people were not used to working with some of the materials. Some people newly employed had never worked on a ship before. Jokes aside, many so called 'dumb people', learned a lot of new skills real fast.

Bob Clark and a guest in the doorway to the stern deck.
Note the sprayed insulation and the new bar.

Estimates of time were off. Many time-consuming jobs—such as fitting 37 toilets—took days, not hours as planned. The fact that some of the fitters employed had never cut, sawed or drilled aluminum before boarding the ship was dealt with.

Some just never learned the new skills needed so they were used as helpers for the skilled trades people.

Shipboard terminology was a whole new lingo for many aboard. I remember a pipe fitter having trouble finding the Engine Room, he kept asking where the basement was so he always got a runaround from the others in the know. For us old timers we just grinned and wondered how you could get lost on a ship that was only 108 feet long.

None of us would ever openly admit our first days on board any vessel were spent sorting ourselves out as to where the bow or the stern was and what all the places in between were with all these funny sounding names. There was the local lad (a clean-up boy), who did not take kindly to being told to go to the shaft compartment one day since he was a hard worker. He did not want to be fired because he needed his job. He cornered me and asked me if I would try to put a good word in for him as he had worked under me a few times already and I had told him he was doing a good job. It seems he had been told by the jokers—every job has them—that the shaft compartment was the office you got sent to when you were being fired.

The shaft compartment on the **Canadian Empress** is the section of the ship that the two drive shafts of the ship run through. It is also where the entire ship's stores are kept. A large storeroom for many things for the lack of a better name.

Another lad had heard some old sea stories from his uncle and so he did not trust working in the shaft compartment with a bunch of strange, rough looking men. But, all things said, we had fun as we worked.

One day another new helper tracked me down to inform me I was needed by Bob Clark to help fit the chimney on the roof. After some confusion it was translated that I was not required on the roof of the building that housed the ship. I was required on the top deck of the ship to help fit the ship's smoke stack. It was being built to tip over and lay on the deck so that the ship would pass under the low bridges of the canal system. After a few good laughs and some hard work the mounting hardware was installed and another job was passed off as completed and ready to be painted by others.

Some of the young ladies from the ship's first crew had never worked around any place like a shipyard before and the daily events were a whole new learning experience for them. College was one thing but a boat yard was a whole new game. Some learned more than just new words.

To help this first ship's crew make up for their lost sailing wages because the ship was not ready, Bob Clark put them to work on the ship as helpers, cleaners and gophers.

The new female ship's crew was ready to quit real fast and Bob Clark could not understand why. He was trying everything possble to keep everyone happy. In his style, he asked the girls point blank what their problem was. He soon found out about the jokes the yard people were handing his greenhorn staff. We had an electrician who kept telling the girls he was working in the niggers nest (a very old term for the crew quarters from the days of square riggers). He even offered to bring in some candles so they could see to go down with him and see where their new hammocks would go. They had been told they would have bunks and showers, not hammocks and slop pails

We had a laugh or two as we worked for even I got conned and was taken off-guard but good.

One of the new deck hands, who filled in as helper, wanted to become a marine engineer in the future so Bob Clark let him work in the engine room to help with the fitting out of the ship. A very good place to learn all the valve locations, controls and such that an engineer must know by heart, even in the dark, if necessary.

I had heard of Kim but never "met Kim" even on this small ship. One late night I was fitting a plate in the engine room area, when in the poor light, someone's backside backed into my working area blocking the little light that I had to see by. Without thinking twice I just took my hand and pushed the invading backside out of my way. To my shock and total surprise a female voice in the near dark said, "You do that again mister and I will break your arm". Kim was not boy Kim, but a girl Kim, and she had felt I was making improper gestures. In a minute or two we all had a good laugh. She may have been a young lady but she did a man's work with great respect from all who worked around her that fall. Her dad, a river tugboat captain based in Kingston and Montréal had trained his daughter well to work on ships with men.

There is a major difference between a carpenter who frames houses and a shipwright. You just don't nail or screw any thing down like you can when you build a house or a motel of wood. Wood is easy to fasten to. On a ship built of metal construction you have to drill a hole first and sometimes you even have to tap threads into the hole to fit a machine screw, or mount a bolt to hold or fasten something. Not everything is square or plumb aboard a vessel either.

Every 2 foot by 4 foot tin deck head panel took 15 to 25 holes and 15 to 25 screws or pop rivets to fasten it up. And this was after you had glued a block of sound-dampening fibreglass on the back with sticky, smelly fireproof glue. If you were very careful you did not break another drill bit as it would stick in the aluminum, burr up or just snap. Sometimes you would drill one hole per every new bit. Now and again you ran a lucky streak and maybe drilled a hundred holes without snapping a bit.

The screws are stainless which means they will not rust but the heads twist off easy if the holes are not drilled to the right size and the fit is too tight for the screw to cut its way into the hole. The experience was ever changing.

I started one day as a labourer and the next day I was a fitter with two helpers when the yard and Bob Clark realized I had three years shipbuilding experience in the shipyards in Kingston. Some people with the yard were surprised to learn that I could even read the drawing and work alone. Some never related to the fact that I had built the model from the same drawing that they were using.

In my past, I had enjoyed the art of being a loftsman in the Kingston Shipyard plus I had been building all types of models for over thirty years. So working from and reading plans was not a venture for me. A loftsman is the person who translates the ships drawing into full size wooden patterns and templates. These patterns and templates are used by fitters for the laying out of the vessel's plates or frames for the right size for cutting or shaping Those of you who walked Expo 67 in Montréal and toured the Ontario Pavilion, will remember big cigar shape tubes that formed the main structure. I am one of two people who laid out the steel for all those big tapering cigar shape tubes that made it such a special place. That is another story for some other day.

For the next three weeks I, and a few other fitters, worked non-stopped. What we called 24/7. Twenty four hours, seven days a week.

Bob Clark and the yard even arranged that we had our meals at a local restaurant at no cost to us and it stayed open late at night just to feed us .

When we were too tired to work, rather than drive back to Kingston each night where a lot of the fitters lived, a distance of 20 plus miles, we just hung a note on a empty stateroom door, and told someone when to wake us up and then crashed in a new bunk in our bedrolls.

My wife and son would bring me changes of fresh clothes. A swim off the dock was as good as a shower for the water was still warm.

There were miles of welding and wiring being done and all had to be checked and tested before we could do some of our work. Plus there were hundreds of feet of steel bulkheads, panels and trim metals to be custom cut and fitted into place without damage to the special vinyl finished surfaces.

We drilled thousands of holes to route the pipes and wires for the electricians and pipe fitters, plus thousands and thousands more holes for all those thousands

of screws and pop rivets that hold everything in place, including all the tin ceilings.

When a stateroom was walled in, then came all the little things that make up the total package. Bunks, night table, window frames, curtain hardware, vanity cabinets, sinks, lights, switches, doors, speakers plus many other things that add up quickly in total labour time required to complete the detailing.

Bob Clark had a good relationship with the yard. He called in some friends who did a yeomen's job working after their regular job and on weekends just to get everything in place. This flexablity could or would not have worked with other building yards. That was one more reason it was built where it was.

WE GOT IT ALMOST DONE

The ship, when finished was as planned. She drew 4 feet 9 inches of water. She had a beam of 30 feet and a length overall of 108 feet plus she had a freeboard height of 21 feet 6 inches with masts and stack laid down on the deck.

Bridges on the Rideau Canal were built to have a clearance of 22 feet at mean water level. As mentioned before the stack and the masts were designed to fold down on the deck. With the mast raised the ship had a height of 33 feet 6 inches.

The ship was designed to hold 6,260 gallons of fresh water, 6,260 gallons of sewage, 2,900 gallons of fuel, and 7,550 gallons of ballast water if required. The ballast water in the tanks, plus the fresh water or seawater could be used for fire fighting purposes if ever required.

The two main drives were Volvos; light duty diesel, commercial engines weighing in at 2.5 tons each.

They produce 365-shaft horsepower at 1800 rpm. These engines turn shafts that are 22 feet long and swing wheels (propellers) that are 36 inches in diameter with 25 inches pitch. The engines' exhausts are directed under water through sea chests in the bottom of the vessel, one on each side, about mid-ship just forward of the side embarkation doors.

The exhaust sea chests are just big boxes built to the bottom of the ship that are full of holes to let water flow in or the exhaust flow out. The though-hull fittings are connected to the many manifolds, pipes and valves that supply seawater to the pumps used to ballast the ship.

Just forward of the main engines are a pair of the same type engines driving the generators that put out

135 KW, 3-phase electricity, with a 10% overload rating; enough power to operate a small town.

The exhaust pipes from the two engines wind across the engine then up through the ship, and out through the smokestack via sound-reducing mufflers hidden in the stack.

On the front of each generator engine is a hydraulic pump that drives the bow thruster that is controlled by a joystick in the bridge and one slave on each of the ships bridge wings.

With the twin screws and the thruster, one can move the ship directly sideways which is very handy in manoeuvering the ship to small docks, in and out of the locks.

With the large side area of the ship and the shallow draft one can have their hands full as the wind tries to control the ship's movements at times. The captain and the mate masterly ply these devices and calmly create another docking that is enjoyable to all.

Remember The Regulations,
That Changed The Construction Of Ships

As you walk though the ship you notice a solid sound, not a tin-canny sound that many come to think of when they think of aluminium ships or boats.

What gives this result are the many tons of the yellow magnesium chloride cement coating that were trowelled on the decks about 1 inch thick. This is a good and bad thing.

A   it quiets the ship down.

B   it is a form of fireproofing for the aluminum decks.

C   it adds a level and smooth surface to the ship's decks for the tile or carpet floors to be applied to.

D   but it also was the cause of major problems for all fitters. Inexperience delayed work. Screws did not hold well in the material. For some items fastened to it, you were forced to drill and tap the deck plate. The nature of the material dulled the bits very quickly.

Once again the best-laid plans will always crumble and always at the wrong time and for all the wrong reasons.

Murphy's Law Again.
It Always Shows Up In Any Shipyard

" What?", you say ! ! !.

The Canadian Empress is a Canadian built ship but many of her parts came from all over the world. All the interior bulkheads on the ship were created in Sweden of a special vinyl coated surface, bonded to steel sheeting panels with a solid compressed core of fiberglass 1 or 2 inches thick between the two metal skins. Special locking strips secure the panels into solid walls.

These panels with their great fireproofing, sound-deadening design have proven to be very functional. They make durable and attractive wall surfaces. They have prove to be very effectived for blocking sound.

The problem was an old one. European and North American engineering drawings are not drawn or read the same way. Just a bit like what happened to Packard cars and their transmissions gears in the Fifties when they were made in England I am told, to reduce cost. Another story some day.

Those bulkhead panels mentioned above became a nightmare for all as we now saw the fun begin.

None of the panels would fit. That's right folks somehow, when it became time to drop those panels into place they were found to be the wrong length.

Thanks to the powers that be, someone erred on the side of too long. Someone had missed the detailed notes about the 1 +/- 1/4 inch of the yellow magnesium chloride cement coating that had to be trowelled on the decks first before the tracks for the panels could be fitted.

On the deckhead is a channel that the top of the bulkhead panels fit up into and then the bottom of the panel drops into a channel fastened to the deck. As the different panels were fitted side-by-side and clipped together, we ended up with a solid insulated metal wall system.

There is a off-white pattern on the vinyl surface for inside the staterooms and showers. As well it was used in the crew quarters. The sections of wall that face the companionways have a cream color pattern on the surface.

Those that were used or faced into the Grand Saloon were surfaced in a rosewood pattern. The wheelhouse was done in a light white oak effect.

As I said, the fun began.

Jigsaws were used to custom cut each panel to be fitted to suit the different heights and openings around the windows and other places as well as to suit their location with regard to the steel support pillars hidden in the companionway's bulkheads. They had to be cut to provide openings for the electrical switches, lights and speaker panel openings.

The $29.00 to $39.00 'do it yourself' grade jigaws lasted three days to a week at most, if you were lucky.

Those tools were never made to be used and worked hard all day long. Most fitters never used a jigsaw more than once or twice a month before, on any other type of job. Soon the yard owners or we fitters ourselves went out and purchased industrial grade jigsaws and drills at $200.00 plus each, a lot of money for a tool even in these days. They were worth every cent. I still have mine.

Remember that 2-inch thickness of the wall panels? Well Murphy remembered it as well. You see, a metal cutting jigsaw blade cuts about 2 1/8 to 2 1/4 inches deep, depending on who manufactured it.

To the unskilled or the not-so-careful operator the blade would bind, then it would jump, or hit the back skin of the panels and you had another broken or a bent blade.

Very shortly the new blade supply was gone. No one had planned for hundreds of feet of extra metal cutting that was needed to install all the wall panels of the ship.

"No metal cutting jigsaw blades in Gananogue or Kingston," was the word for several workdays.

The yard sent out drivers with cash in their pockets to scour the countryside of Eastern Ontario, one east and one west, to visit every lumber yard and hardware store for miles around.

They acquired every type of metal cutting blade in stock from any source they could find that would fit our different saws.

The good Bosch blades were the best but at $1.50 each it got expensive for the yard. Sometime you used two blades just to cut a sheet to length.

Soon only a chosen few people were allowed to cut the steel skin panels not only because they had

the job skill for that type of layout work but they also had the feel to avoid blade breakage or damage to the panel surface as much as possible.

Some days we got to the point a blade would last for 3 or 4 hours of steady, slow, noisy, cutting work. Talk about having and using goodluck charms.

Another delay was the plastic protection film that the panels were coated with, that was both a help and a nuisance. It would have been better if it was thicker that's for sure.

Some times the film balled up under the shoe of the jigsaw as you cut, making the saw stick, worse still it melted to the blades which helped to bind the blades.

Other times it would release and fall off the panel and you would lose all your carefully laid out marking of where you had planned to cut.

Then we had to use masking tape to protect the surface and to create a new surface to re-lay out the cutting plan. Great fun and games.

Some times when you went to strip it off before installing the panel in place it would not release. Ever try to remove wallpaper that has been hung for some time. Zip!!! One sheet will come clean but the next you pick, and pick, and pick, even though no two were the same but they all went up at the same time.

The heat from friction caused by the cutting action of the blades would cause the film to melt and bond to the vinyl at the edge of the cut.

Some days it would almost drive you to drink as almost every sheet required a whole new game plan to get it laid out, cut, stripped and mounted.

You had to use a sharpened section of pipe that was driven down or up the length of the core of the panels to clear a passage way to route the wiring to the different light or switch openings.

Just like drilling for oil, you never always came out in the right place or the friction of the compressed fiberglass core would bind the pipe on you. Some not nice words were spoken by a few of the trades at times.

The many different brands of saw blades, cutting edges and styles made it a challenge for all that worked with them.

The ladies of the work groups, both the employed ones and the friends of Bob, got the job to go into each stateroom to do the detailing of removing the film. Sometimes long fingernails have a use, great for picking at all the film.

It was found that not all the panels were stripped of the film before installing for, at one time, it was planned to leave it in place until after the deckhead panels were fitted and painted. That proved not to be a good plan. They forgot the panels fitted into a track top and bottom, which covered some of the panels' surface. Even today, as I work in the ship, I find little sections of the film still in place after all these years.

The end results were as planned and the material has preformed with great success for all these years.

Drill bits were fun too. Even the industrial grade drill bits died from overwork. Think of how many tin panels are required to cover all the deckheads of the three levels of the ship that have them. Now count the holes that have to be drilled and the number of screws. More fun than counting sheep.

Before you fall asleep, think of behind all those bulkheads and deckheads. Think of the fittings that you will never see that are held in place with a screw or two or three or four. Nails do not work on metal ship surfaces for the fastening of anything.

Want some more fun? Sit in the Grand Saloon and study that beautiful tin plate ceiling and think of all the different parts that make it up. Now, have you ever put up something like that before? Well, neither had any of the work crew.

The product had not been on the market as a new material since before the Second World War.

It was a fit-and-learn process and when they first put it up they used pop rivets so as to have a smoother finish and look.

Big Problem

Every rivet had to be drilled out to relocate the panels. Murphy's law had struck again.

We did not have a wood ceiling surface to work with, to lay out the total area as a grid first as they did in 'the good old days' when this material was used every day.

We relearned by the school of hard knocks with a learning curve that involved trials and errors.

If you are a little off, who will ever see a thirty-second or sixteenth of an inch. Not a big deal.

Not a major problem, that is, till you add up 8 or 10 of those little slips and you find you are a full half inch or more adrift.

Whole days of work were wasted as some of the fitters struggled with the learning curve problems.

It soon became the standard smart cracks whenever anyone was seen with a panel in hand. "How many times did you measure that?" "Where are your chalk lines?" "Are you sure you know what you are doing?" Everyone loves the wise crackers especially when things are behind the eightball of time.

Good craftsmen take pride in their work. Ribbing hurts productivity but it happens. In time, as you learn, the pride returns.

Like any major job, the detail work flowed up the chain to one or two top-level fitters. Soon new tricks were developed that others had discovered many, many years ago when the last tin ceiling was installed by building masters. It is almost an art form when you study it closely. Those few skilled people have an eye, a feel, for what is right. As my dad would say, "They could walk, talk, and chew tobacco at the same time."

Pressure is the story of drill bits. Too much pressure on the drill 'snap', the little diameter drill bit breaks easily. Too little, you just over-heat and burn the tip. Too much pressure can make the bit slip sideways on you, or you bind it in a hole—more broken bits. The soft aluminium just grabs and binds the bit easily.

To top this all off, it was found that at different places drill bits or a screw had cut a wire in behind the panels. Some times a simple repair. At other times a major rip out, replacement or a rerouting of the wires for a safer life span. For some places the screws just had to be where they were.

More trips to the shore stores for replacement bits and more screws, but we got it finished.

While all these fun jobs were taking place we had at the same time a major traffic problem.

The Grand Saloon was just grand for more than it was designed for. Great workshop area. Great storage area, for anything that came on board. In the middle of all this clutter the local carpenter was creating and attempting to mount the bar he had built ashore, plus all the window casings, not to mention the cabinets in the galley. To one side, the electricians had their stands, to hold reels of different wires, as they measured and cut great lengths and then dragged and pulled them, to where they got buried in the bulkheads and behind the many panels.

Think of all the equipment in the galley, its size its shape. At one time it rested or was assembled in the Grand Saloon area too.

Building a ship is just like an ant colony or a bee-hive. Everyone is doing a different job somewhere at the same time, even though there is a master plan and bosses or troubleshooters mix in with the workers to control the ever-changing advance of work. It did not look that way to the inexperienced eye, but it all fell into place. Generally it was later than sooner. Murphy and his Law saw to that.

Then It Became A Job Of Spit, Polish And Shine

Boxes of many different things, that had been hiding in storage for some time came aboard, to complete and dress the ship. What a list of things when you stop and write it all down! Just think of each job description for the crew of the ship. Now think of their needs in materials each day, to perform their many tasks and all possible things that are their responsibility for a safe and enjoyable voyage. It all came aboard and was then fitted into place. A lot could only be tested once in place with everything else.

Life was just like ants at an anthill. One group of ants carted the full boxes aboard. Other ants unpacked, sorted and filled the many places. No one went ashore without a armful of cardboard and packing material for the dumpster.

Finally We Took Her To Kingston

As we sailed away from Gananoque, the Grand Saloon was filled with stacks of mattresses and bedding, including the full load of linens and all the extra changes (three complete sets) as well as all the required spare parts. It was an intersting passage that day as the army of ants moved and placed and readjusted all the items. It was distracting for those who had not been on the river before, plus there was the fleet of boats that followed in a great parade. More new things to look at. That morning was car-pool morning in Kingston for some, for others it was going back to Gananoque, and who had room for whom and at what time.

It was a big push all day, things had to look ship-shape really fast as there was a party scheduled on board that night in Kingston.

But We Made It

A great time for all. Canada had, for the first time in a long time a Canadian-owned and based passenger ship, sailing under the red and white flag, in international waters.

FROM
BOW
TO STERN

GENERAL CONSTRUCTION

As I have detailed in other sections, the ship is of a 'stressed skin of aluminium' construction for several reasons. One, there is a great weight reduction compared to steel with aluminium being about half the weight. Another big factor is the ease of working the material to different shapes and its strength.

A very important factor for a cruise ship owner too is the 'no rust' quality of aluminium. As a passenger, one does not see the ship with all those creative and interesting looking patterns of rusting that happens all over on steel ships. Steel ships rust. They always have and they always will, which only causes many hours of chipping and painting all year long by the crew to control Mother Nature.

There is some steel used in the main construction of the vessel but only in a few specialized places. None is exposed to the weather. One place steel is used is for the support posts between the decks, (see the picture on page 32) but there is not a lot of steel in the main construction of the hull compared to the total mass of the ship.

The vinyl-coated steel doors and bulkhead materials are from Sweden. They are standard marine stateroom doors of a type found on vessels of all types world wide with the lower door section having kick out vents or escape plates and they all sport solid brass lever handles with special keys. Passengers are asked not to take the keys home as Souvenirs. As you walk along the companionways you will notice the round manhole covers in the decks that lead to the different compartments below. These manhole cover plates are operational from both sides above or below and are removable by the average person.

Throughout the ship, the deckhead and area framework of every deck, as well as all the outer hull bulkhead plating and frameworks above the water line including the outside surface of any tanks, were sprayed with a special type of cellulose insulation.

It serves several functions at the same time.

(a) It helps deaden sound.

(b) It also increases fire protection ratings, as it would slow down the heat transfer in the event of a fire.

(c) It also insulates the surfaces to reduce condensation which is ever present in metal ships.

Before it was sprayed in place, all the plastic piping of the hot and cold potable water system was run and clipped into place including the waste water system.

The air conditioning piping system being copper had to be isolated from the aluminium and padded to reduce noise. Wiring of all types was strung through all the webbing, through all the hundreds of drilled holes that each also had plastic grommets fitted to reduce the chance of friction wear spots and/or to also isolates the wires and cables from the aluminium. Most power cables are covered with a bronze braid. The last thing one needs is galvanic action between the different metals.

In areas of large flat surfaces to be coated, pin plates were glued in place first and then after the coating was sprayed on the square 1.5 inch tin plates were pushed onto the pins to help secure the insulation in place for a longer life span.

The builders and crew had a love/hate relationship for the insulation. It sure was an incentive to get it covered though. Every one had what we called shaft cooties (little fluffs of insulation in your hair) till it was all buttoned up. These were named after the shaft compartment deckhead which was one of the busiest and last areas to get covered.

The height varies in the shaft compartment from about 6 feet to about 4 feet going aft, which meant every trip down there for work or for material you would rub or bang your head in the stuff. This is where a lot of small fittings were stored and you went there often.

Every time you drilled a hole overhead the insulation stuff flaked off and fell in your hair, face or down your neck—not nice on a hot day.

On the two stateroom levels as well as the bridge and the crew quarters deckheads you will find the sheet tin stamped deckhead plates as talked about earlier.

The other non-public compartments of the ship have an expanded metal mesh fitted over the insulation to control erosion of it.

For the vertical surfaces other than the vinyl-

coated steel bulkheads, you will find them spray painted with three coats of special fireproof paint, be they of
aluminium or wood material.

An enjoyable feature of each stateroom is the
fact that they all have at least 2 windows that open. The
windows are of a type that you find in some high quality factory built homes, all aluminium. Dark brown
in colour, double-hung safety glass with screens. For
those that want to see the world as a round thing then
staterooms 24 and 25, the premiere suites, are the
rooms to stay in for they have port holes. Staterooms
22 and 23 have them also.

As you see the ship alongside you will notice a
row of smaller portholes below and aft of larger stateroom portholes. These are the ones fitted in the crew
quarters' area of the ship.

Throughout the ship the window casing and
sills, the bunks, the vanities, night tables and the bar
were all created of Canadian maple and finished in a
special early Canadian maple colonial stain finish that
had been created at Upper Canada Village by their
craftsman.

Recycling started on the ship back when it was
built. The shipyard, for it size, had no loft area of a
suitable size to handle the ship's required needs, so a
novel idea was used. A plywood loft floor was created
and painted white.

All the ship's frames and special plates were

lofted on that surface. When that surface was no longer needed, the plywood material that had been used
was unscrewed and lifted. Then it was use to create the
floors of the bunks, a great saving of cost and a major
saving of material from ending up in the dumps.

One thing the old ships had, and that the *Canadian Empress* has a lot of, is brass, brass, and more
brass. It is everywhere. The passengers love it. But
then they don't have to polish it every day.

I have never been able to understand why people like brass, but they do. Maybe it's the shine and
sparkle that in certain light make it look like gold.

There are brass handrails everywhere on the
ship. Rails run the length of the companionways, both
sides, up the stairwells and around the top combings.
Outside the bridge the *Canadian Empress* has a bronze
ship's bell. The bridge doors have brass portholes and
other brass hardware. Even inside the bridge there is
an antique brass Engine Room Telegraph Quadrant.

No, the Telegraph Quadrant is not used to operate the ship, it is just for show in keeping with the
period of the ship's image. The brass taps of the staterooms and door levers add to the classic image of the
ship as well   as the lamps on the stern deck that give
that soft evening light adding to the shine on those two
big spare marine bronze wheels on the bulkhead.

When I sailed as a mate, we loved to leave the
Quadrant levers in full reverse as we headed down the

river when we would leave Montréal. Sooner or later a passenger would stop by the wheelhouse to take a picture or two.

Quadrant levers in full reverse

The brave or the unlearned would ask why the engines were in reverse and with a straight face we would tell them we had to run the ship that way due to the fact we were traveling down river and the current was too fast and that we did not want to arrive in the next port of call ahead of time.

Some people believe anything they are told and took pictures of it that way.

It created great fun when their looks let you know they were not buying that sailors' story. Nowadays I un-

derstand the Bridge is off limits when the ship is underway so I would guess the captain or mate would not get all those fun question that made for great memories and good laughs at the time.

One question that is asked all the time is, "How fast will she go?" Well, the average speed is about 8.5 to 10 knots due to river speed zones. Top speed is about 13 knots when the ship is clear of those control zones. I once recorded 18.6 knots downbound the Richelieu Rapids above Québec City as we rode the tide out and were helped along with a heavy tail wind. On the return trip the next day the storm was still blowing strong, right down the river. We crawled up those same rapids at 4.3 knots. That trip we got in to Three Rivers, Québec, 5 hours late. The trip was slow and painful for Mother Nature laid a storm all day that blew up to 55 knots on the bow.

Generally our passage was designed that we would have an extra hour to kill in that up bound section of passage.

FOREDECK
AND
FOREPEAK

The forward "Observation Area" as listed in the brochures is under the bright yellow canvas canopy on the bow of the ship. To the crew it is called the foredeck.

This area is one of the areas of the ship that also serves many purposes.

If you board or disembark at Kingston you pass up or down the gangway to this deck through the bow embarkation gates. This deck leads through the forward embarkation door to the Ottawa Deck, which is the upper level of staterooms and into the Grand Saloon.

As you look around the foredeck you will notice secured against the bulkhead is the spare anchor. Also you will find a fire station of hose and an axe.

Mounted on the bulkhead too are the storm

The red hand-powered winch and spare anchor

covers for the forward companionway door window as well as the two windows of staterooms 33 and 34.

On the forward area of the deck is the red winch that is used to raise and lower the ship's anchor that hangs ready at all time over the side on the starboard bow of the ship.

At different points on the deck are different coloured pipes that load potable water, fuel and the discharge pipe for the sewage from the holding tanks plus vent pipes from the tanks.

At the bow on the forward mast flies a burgee to

Bow burgee

assist the captain to ascertain the wind direction on the ship's bow.

On the deck are mounted the bollards that hold the heavy lines that secure the ship alongside. To the port side of the stairwell is the black raised seat hatch that opens the way down to the forepeak below.

Here the spare lines for the ship are kept plus the paints that are used to touch up the ship as required.

The inflatable bumpers that protect the ship when

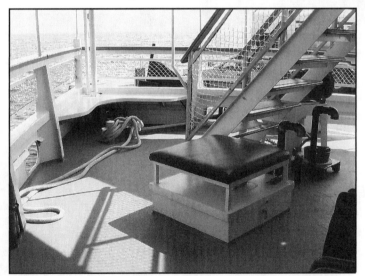

The pipes of the bow and forepeak hatch seat.

alongside are also stored here between dockings. This area also becomes the storage area for the bags of dirty linens and garbage till the ship meets its next service port.

Below the forepeak deck is the forward ballast water tank.

In the centre of the deck is the stairway up to the captain's walk.

The captain's walk is the walkway around the wheelhouse. When the ship is alongside this stairway is open for use by the passengers and all. When underway it is for crew use only as the ship's master and crew must keep a steady eye on the ever-changing water above and below the surface.

Overhead on the supporting pipe framework is the yellow canvas covering with its white and yellow trimmed valance that provides shade and protection for those on the deck.

THE BRIDGE

The captain's walk around the bridge serves as access to the wheelhouse through solid oak doors with their brass portholes and hardware.

Port-side wing area.
Engine controls mounted on the post.
Inflatable life raft on top deck

On the wings are the the wing post, on which are mounted the extra slave controls for the engines and thruster plus a speaker system to the bow and stern decks. The speaker system is to assist the ship handler in giving directions to the crew when docking or departing.

Just outboard at this point one locates the ship's running lights, red for port side and green for starboard in their big brass-coloured cases mounted against the black backboards.

The *Canadian Empress* was designed in such a way that the engine room could be controlled from the wheelhouse. The two main drive engines can be started and operated from up there. In the center of the wheelhouse is the console that holds the ship's wheel that is hydraulically connected to the ship's rudders. On the left side of the console are the port engine instruments, speed/transmission control levers, which are connected

The wheel and bridge console

finds the fold-down chart table on the port side, that stores the charts but also provides a working surface to lay the charts out on. One never knows all the information of all of the river routing.

When the chart table is lowered it uncovers both the main bridge 12-volt and 110-volt power panels and fire and alarm control panels. Against the starboard side are the ship's sound systems and cabinet and the tape decks.

Overhead on the deckhead is the ship's radio, and in the centre is the ship's rudder position indicator plus a pull cord for the whistle, which is mounted on the stack. This whistle was reworked so that it could be operated by compressed air power, not steam power.

Kingston harbor is one of the many places where the compass is way off. There are heavy iron deposits in areas of the riverbed that will sometimes cause the compass to just spin like a top. So now the ship carries a modern GPI unit relegating the radar to a back-up system,

As you step through the fireproof door you enter the quarters of the captain on the starboard side with his locker, desk, vanity, bunk and the ship's safe.

To the port side are the bunks of the mate and the chief engineer, which are mounted to the bulkhead, one over the other. The mate and chief have their own lockers, but they share a vanity which also hold their life jackets. All three officers share the common bridge shower and toilet/ bathroom.

by cables to that engine in the engine room. On the right hand side is the starboard set for the starboard engine and in the centre of the console is the ship's compass. Between it and the ship's spoked wooden wheel, is the little joystick that controls the hydraulic driven bow thruster.

In front of the console on the forward bulkhead below the windows are the port and starboard control panels for the auxiliary engines which control the generators or the hydraulic thruster pumps. One unit is running all the time to make electric power for the ship. To the right of the starboard panel is the radar unit and overhead of this is the Global Position Indicator.

Against the wheelhouse bulkhead that separates it from the quarters of the captain, mate and engineer, one

Even in the wheelhouse and officers quarters we see the cream-coloured, tinplate deckheads and the English wool carpet underfoot. The bulkheads under the windows are the same material as used throughout the ship but are finished to look like light white oak.

Under the chart table is the boatswain's locker that holds signal flags, and other safety-at-sea equipment.

The sound cabinet holds the equipment that pipes the sound into the ship's speaker system through the whole ship as well as the emergency public address system.

The staterooms have two channels while the common areas enjoy only one channel.

Beside and above this cabinet is mounted all the licenses required for the ship as well as the ship-to-shore phone.

All Stop

TOP DECK

The top deck holds many things.

It is a great area from which to view the river sights as well as from the bow and stern deck areas. This area is enclosed by wire fence with its wooden handrail. From the sides also hang, at different locations, the international red life rings. One never knows if and when they will be needed. At different locations are speakers for the sound system of the ship. This deck is also the second-most social centre of the ship.

In the centre to aft section of the deck is the raised area between the two strong backs. (see glossory) It is here the shuffleboard court is laid out with it's scoreboard mounted on the aft side of the smoke stack.

Forward of the stack in the area behind the wheel-house, is the giant checkerboard with its giant-sized markers.

Outboard of the strong backs with their lockers is plenty of area for the many deck chairs and lounges.

Forward to the roof of the wheelhouse

Aft of the wheelhouse on the starboard side, is the ship's boat. It is a classic fibreglass reproduction of a 'Thousand Island Rowing Skiff', bright yellow in colour and will seat two crew members.

On the port side are the red Carling floats (life rafts) with their reflective white strips and the two inflatable life rafts in their white cocoons.

Just aft of these positions one finds more port and starboard boarding gates to be used at some of the different docking sites along the river. The river downstream from Montréal can have a great shift in water levels due to tides and winds; as well, the docks are all at different heights above the water.

Top deck looking aft

Each side of the wheelhouse are the steps coming up from the captain's walk. Right behind the wheelhouse are two large white boxes. In the port side one are the ship's 12-volt batteries and special controllers that provide the emergency lighting for the whole ship as well as power for all the bridge navigation equipment. In the other one are the extra life jackets (required by law) so that if people were out of their stateroom and an emergency happened, they would not have to return to their rooms below-deck to get one.

There are also the two life jackets that are stored in every room in the bottom of the vanity. Staterooms 24 and 25 have 3 jackets each, because those rooms will accommodate three people.

On top of the wheelhouse one finds a mast that holds the ship's forward navigation lights. Here flies the flag of the national waters the ship is sailing in. In American waters the vessel shows an American flag for respect of that nation. To not do so would at least be an insult to the American people or at worst a declaration of war under international laws. In Canadian waters the ship will, at times, fly the flag of the port of call or a flag of the harbour that it is in. When cruising the provincial waters of Ontario or Québec, their flag is shown. There is also the array of different antennas for the ship's radios, radar, phones and GPI systems.

Outboard of the strong backs, along the shuffleboard court, are lockers for the deckhands to store their ramps and boxes for the gangway as well as the big rubber fenders.

Inside the large smoke stack, which is painted in the company's internationally registered colours, are the two mufflers for the exhaust pipes that come up from the two auxiliary engines. On the front side of the stack is the converted steam whistle. Beside the stack are two more large white boxes that hold more of the life jackets as well as the air compressor that supplies the air for the whistle.

Outboard the port side of the white boxes is the 'Charlie Noble'. This is the funnel that drafts air from the galley.

Aft of the shuffleboard court is a fence that safely ends the shuffleboard elevated court. It is the location of the aft mast that carries the company flag and navigation light. This is the light shown when the ship is at anchor.

At the aft top deck, above the top of the stairwell lead-ing up from the stern deck, one finds a locker for the storage of the skeet shooting equipment. Mounted on the port stern rail in the corner behind the safety rail from the stairwell is the launcher for clay pigeons for skeet shooting . Forward of this area on the port side near the top of the stairwell is another of the many fire stations.

One can reach every point of the ship with a fire hose from their many locations as required by law. One location is tested at each fire drill and is logged in the ship's log of such facts.

Mounted on the stern above the stern deck and hanging out over the water is the ship's main flag mast. This one carries the ship's national flag. Below it is the white stern light in its large brass-coloured case.

STERN DECK

Around the brim of the stern one finds a decorative band of the same yellow and white canvas awning edging that was fitted around the bow, to complete the finished look of the ship. Here, we also find both another port and starboard side boarding gates, to be used at some of the different docking sites along the river as well being the main point of embarking ship's stores. The three bollards that hold the heavy lines that secure the ship alongside are mounted on the deck.

Under the stairwell to the top deck is the liquor lock-up for the bar that holds the reserve supply so the ship does not run dry of important things like beer, ale and wine. On the bulkhead is a beautiful antique brass lamp with its crackled bubble glass shade that provides soft evening light for the area. Beside that hangs one of the many life rings found around the ship. This one is popular with photo takers.

Beside the sliding door from the Grand Saloon, on the bulkhead, one finds a classic red Canadian mailbox. It is the old style that says Royal Canadian Mail. Just above this is

Royal Canadian mailbox, lights and life ring

another bubble glass antique brass lamp.

Starboard of the light are the two stern windows of the Grand Saloon. Mounted to the bulkhead, as required by law, are the two spare marine bronze wheels that have been kept polished by the crew.

The stairwell to the upper deck enjoys a classic old style wooden screen door. The railings and post around the stern are fitted with Velcro® to hold the removable screen panels because at certain times of the year Mother Nature makes

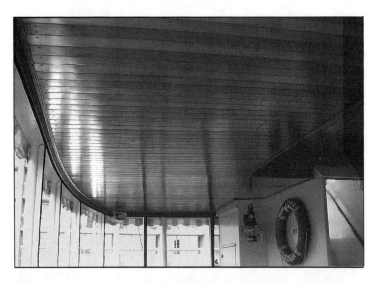

Cedar deckhead of the Stern Deck

bugs and not all enjoy their shortlived lifestyles.

Overhead, one finds the classic oil-treated, cedar board deckhead with its hundreds of brass screws. There is also some of this structure applied to the stern bulkhead with its oak kickplate below the railings. This makes for a charm-

ing setting as the soft breezes surround you while you take in the views of the evening in the wicker deck chairs of old, with a long cool drink in hand.

The wicker deck chairs

GRAND SALOON

The Grand Saloon, the Lounge, the Big Room—no matter what you call it—it is the social centre of the ship. It is always open to the passengers for their varied uses. The room contains three doors as well as the staircase from the lower St. Lawrence Deck. Aft is the heavy wood-framed sliding glass door that leads out onto the Stern Deck, and forward there are two doors. Port side is the solid fireproof steel door that leads into the galley with its shiny brass kick plate.

The remaining door is a fancy one, an antique pine door with sandblasted glass and antique brass hardware. This door had a history of many years prior to being used in its present location. This is the door that leads forward into the Ottawa Deck companionway.

Like the companionways with their brass railings, you will find those same brass railings coming up into the grand stairwell and around the top of the cream-painted wooden framework of the stairwell opening.

The brass rails

The railing not only adds safety to the opening but caps the view.

This framework also contains some of the ship's library of games and books in a fitted bookshelf opening built into the inboard side. The other set of library shelves is mounted on the bulkhead just to the port of the forward doorway between it and the galley doorway.

On the forward bulkhead, just beside the door that opens into the Ottawa Deck companionway, one finds the water fountain for those who wish a cool drink of water. Outboard of this is the buffet counter. Here one finds coffee or hot water for tea, which is always ready, even in the wee hours of the morn, plus two chilled juice dispensers, quietly bubbling all the time.

The Bar

The large square windows of both port and starboard sides of the Grand Saloon are dressed with velvet curtains and the deck has its own pattern of a period carpet in keeping with the look of the ship. These two features enhance the rosewood paneling of the room's bulkheads.

Just forward of the grand staircase is the maple-inlaid wooden dance floor, if the evening entertainment is music and the sounds create the desire to dance.

Other than the pictures and awards that colour the walls, one would have to list the bar in the port stern area as the most outstanding feature of the room. The cabin-

etry for the ship's bar is built of maple and finished in the same colonial stain that is used throughout the ship. The tambours of the cabinets roll up when the bar is open to display the many choices of liquor and glasses against the soft lights and antique mirrors of their interior. The bar is complete with beer and wine coolers, plus state of the art dispensers for spirits and mixers.

The working area of stainless steel sinks and counters, as required for a complete bar, fit under the serving bar.

From the passenger side of the bar one can see the brass foot and elbow railings that draw your eye as you enjoy the drinks the bartender created for you. The bar is a stand up type but it also has three high-armed bar stools for those who want to stay a while and enjoy the view from on high and/or buttonhole the bartender with questions of the sights about the river as it flows by.

The round tables of the Grand Saloon with their massive, antique, black cast iron bases serve a multitude of purposes for the room. Their edge sections are made to fold down and out of the way to create a square shape, which al-

The Tin Ceiling

lows the crews to set them up in many configurations for the two different sizes of tables. There is meal time, party time, game time, tea time and entertainment time. Flip, flip, flip, and the square tables are round for an enjoyable card game. Changes can be made to suit the needs for more space for 6 or 8 at a dining table. Sometime they only flip two sides up or down to suit the needs of the day or event.

Surrounding the tables one finds the Canadian maple chairs with their soft green seat pads that com-

plete the seating layouts for the many happenings that take place each day, These too are finished in the colonial stain.

Overhead one sees the square, hanging, antique glass lampshades of years gone by. Their wood frames, that cap the glass boxes, are hung on chains to compensate for the movement of the ship. There is also a small section of track lighting to spotlight the nightly entertainment.

As one stands at the buffet and fixes a coffee or tea, one can look in the mirror with its elegant antique frame that is mounted on the bulkhead. It is fitting for it complements the pictures and frames of Queen Victoria on the aft bulkhead or of Sir John A. on the galley bulkhead. Macdonald's picture has a stately place near the galley.

Awards

Sir John A. Macdonald, Canada's first Prime Minister

Queen Victoria

His picture could have been closer to the bar as he was known to be more of a connoisseur of the spirits than of the foods.

In keeping with the rest of the ship, the large window sills are of Canadian maple, stained and finished in the same colonial maple that is used throughout the ship, complementing the bar.

Surrounding the room, between the windows with their velvet drapes, are the fluted wooden columns, which are painted cream with gold flutes. Mounted on these columns are ornate, Victorian style cast brass gooseneck wall sconces. The fluted and frosted glass globes of these wall sconces provide a soft luminous light for the Grand Saloon. Come evening they bring more opulence to the room as they cast a warm glow on the cream coloured panels of the ornately designed and laid out embossed tin plate deckhead with its vaulted centre section.

All these fixtures complete the picture with the attractive deep rosewood finish of the special vinyl-coated bulkhead panels.

Another one of the Saloon's features is its piano. This instrument is short in height, a modern black piano that one would find in a night club but it has a trick of its own that has proven to be a delight to many.

The trick is, that it does not look like the player piano that it is. It has a tape cassette-driven player unit, which creates some fun times for those good, or bad, who play pianos. The piano is a standard piano but it has electronic control units that allow one to record the movement of the keys and pedals. With the flip of a switch it can replay the recorded works of others. In my days aboard the ship we would tell the passengers the piano came with a ghost of its own as they saw the keys go up and down, making music with no one sitting on the bench. Many are amazed as they just watch with their mouths open as it replays their little ditties they had just played with the same missed or flat notes. For those who need to know, the piano recording equipment is controlled and hidden in the bar.

Beside the piano on the bulkhead was the location for the Grand Saloon entertainment sound system.

In the winter of 2002-2003 the sound equipment was relocated to the port side bulkhead, forward of the windows near the galley.

To add history to history the traveler has real confirmation of the past. Mounted over the water fountain for all to set their timepiece with, a plaque that reads.

Ship's clock from the S.S. RAPIDS PRINCE
In service from 1911 to 1951

Donated to the M.V. Canadian Empress
From the marine collection of
River Captain Fred Roney 1923 - 2002

Above the clock in the picture on page 79 one sees a more detailed image of the ornate, Victorian-style cast brass gooseneck wall sconces. The fluted and frosted glass globes of these wall sconces provide the soft luminous light for the Grand Saloon in the evenings.

Above all else, meals are enjoyed in grand style, and the bartender stocks a very good selection of wines to suit all taste.

A table set for six awaits the guests

THE GALLEY

Sailors the world over will tell you the bridge is the brain of the ship, but passengers want to know about the galley.

In the galley you will find a very compact and complete ship's kitchen. At times they have to feed 79 people, three times a day, plus all those snacks enjoyed in between that generate their share of joy to those who enjoy them, and a challenge to the staff who prepare them and for the clean-up crew. That's a lot of dishes and food preparation, pots, pans and trays to clean and store.

For starters the room has a main sink, a dishwasher, as well as a staff hand-wash sink. Cleanliness is important in food safety. They prepare and bake fresh rolls in a large proofing oven and grill your bacon on the salamander, (a technical name for a big electric barbeque). Bread is turned into toast with an auto toaster, while over on the grill, pancakes or eggs are cooking. On the counters are stacks of plates and at the same time glasses being filled with juice in a room that is

Gally stove and refrigerator

less then 10 feet x 11 feet. I forgot to tell you it contains the oak cupboards with shelving and doors for all the other dishes.

The big fridge takes a large block of space with its wide double doors. There is even one of those modern standard home staple kitchen appliances that any chef is lost with out—the microwave oven. This one sits on a wall shelf where everyone can reach it in their time of need.

The pantry

In the 5 feet wide pantry behind the galley, are the two freezers for the frozen foods plus all the shelving that holds all the dry foods. This metal shelving also holds the mixing bowls, pans, pots plus the boxes, bags and jars of dry food.

To help the chef and galley staff keep a cool head the overhead fans suck the heat and vapours outboard. The Charlie Noble on the top deck sucks the hot air from the galley as the air flows over it.

All in all it's a very compact but highly efficient galley that puts out great creative meals and snacks. No space is wasted for behind the galley door are the racks for the serving trays. Even the back of the galley door is used to hang the first aid kits. People do get hurt at times and the crew is ready and trained for that too.

COMPANIONWAYS

The companionways are the hallways of a ship.

The bulkheads are finished with the cream colour that complements the light brown oak look of the stateroom doors. Along both sides are mounted the ever-present brass handrails, for safety.

Mounted along the length are the hall lights, both the 110-volt as well as the 12-volt backup emergency lighting.

On the St Lawrence Deck, (lower passenger deck) the companionway runs almost the length of the ship. It starts near the bow outside staterooms 24 and 25 and passes along 23 and 22 before one must climb the four steps to where it widens out for the stairwell up to the Ottawa Deck with its fire door. Under this stairwell is the stairwell down into the crew quarters where one would again pass through another fire door.

At this point we also find one of the many fire stations on the ship with hose and water valve plus a fire axe.

St. Lawrence Deck looking towards the bow

Just before the crew quarters' stairwell one finds one of two main linen closets on this deck. This one supplies the twelve forward staterooms. The other is beside the Corner Store and supplies the aft twelve staterooms. These are the linen closets that hold everything from fresh towels, clean sheets, to the vacuum cleaners and all the other material used to restore the rooms each day. They are restocked nightly from the ship's main store in the shaft compartment as required.

Next, as we move aft is the Corner Store, which is the front of the purser's office. Here one can purchase souvenirs of the trip and settle shipboard accounts. There is even a little box for complaints or suggestion on the bulkhead. I might add they have helped keep the ship in the good shape it operates in.

Across the way is the carpeted staircase with brass handrails to the Grand Salon with its sliding fire door. Next the main companionway is joined from the embarkation companionways that lead to the Port and Starboard side embarkation doors.

Just inside the starboard door one finds the door of the Purser's Office. On the port side is an alcove where the doors are under the Grand Saloon staircase. These lead down into the Engine Room or the Shaft Compartment. Located in the small alcove, by these doors, is the ship's ironing board and iron for all to use. Outside stateroom 5 is another fire station.

Corner Store

On the stern bulkhead outside staterooms 1 and 2 in an ornate glided frame are the words spoken by Shillane Clark (then age 11), niece of the Founder, for the christening of the ship in Kingston On May 8, 1982.

Christening Canadian Empress

May the Eighth,
Nineteen Hundred & Eighty-two

Almighty God, Who Guided Noah
In The
Building of an Ark,
And Calmed The Raging Sea,
We Call Upon You to Bless
Those Who Have Prepared This Ship
For Service,

And To Protect And Preserve
Those Who Sail In Her,
And Surround Them With Your
Loving Care.

I Hereby Christen This Ship -
"Canadian Empress"

Shillane Clark (age 11),
Niece of Founder

The young ladies on their day of glory
Shillane Clark And Canadian Empress

The companionway of the upper deck, which is called the Ottawa Deck, runs from the foredeck into the Grand Saloon. One passes the four staterooms 35, 34, 33 and 32, before one must climb the four steps to where it widens out for the stairwell up from the St. Lawrence Deck. Here one finds another linen closet that supplies the eight staterooms of the deck. Mounted on the side of the closet is another fire station. Beside the closet is the ice cube machine that provides ice for all the needs of the ship.

Along both sides are mounted the ever-present brass handrails with the lights both 110 and 12-volt. Just before one passes through the frosted glass door in the

Grand Saloon is the antique mirror for one to check their appearance before making their entrance.

Overhead throughout all the companionways one will find mounted speakers that carry the sound and messages of the ship as well as several of the red alarm bells they hope they will only hear during drills.

Foreward Ottawa Deck

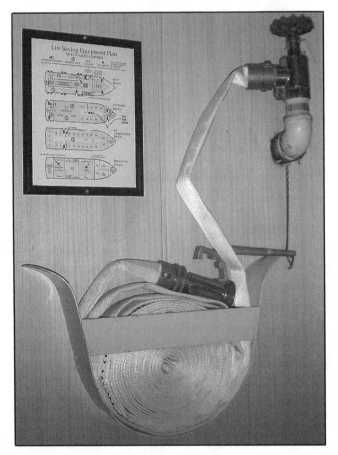

A Fire Station Ottawa Deck

One of the many ornate wall lights

THE STATEROOMS

Stateroom 24, a premier suite

Aboard the *Canadian Empress* there are four classes of staterooms. First there are the 20 St. Lawrence class staterooms, which cover most of the St. Lawrence Deck. Then there are the 8 Ottawa class staterooms of the Ottawa Deck. The two corner staterooms in the stern of the St. Lawrence Deck are listed as the Sterling class. The two most forward staterooms on the St. Lawrence are classed as the Premier Suites.

No matter which stateroom one enjoys, they all have two windows or portholes that open. Their decks are covered with richly coloured, floral designed carpets, from England.

All but four staterooms have one fixed bunk and one Pullman (fold up) bunk and there is a drawer fitted under the fixed bunk,

Fixed bunk to the left and Pulman on the right

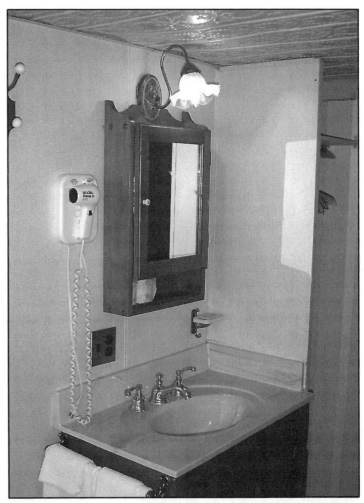

Vanity

A nightstand is fitted to the bulkhead, between the windows. At one time each held an ashtray but not any more. The ship is now smoke free. Now it just holds the famous Gideon Bible that travelers of the world look for.

Vanities have marble type tops with solid brass taps on the sinks. All Taps were replaced a few years ago.

On the walls are mounted medicine cabinets,

above the vanities, to hold all your little goodies, complete with a mirror in the door. These cabinets were custom created of maple and finished in a colonial maple stain, as are the nightstand and window frames. Over the nightstand is the speaker system of the ship, which allows two different channels of music, which can be controlled by channel selection and volume. For the passengers' safety and to meet the law, even if the unit is turned off, the system is designed so that all emergency announcements will be heard loud and clear.

The rooms are fitted with Victorian style wall lamps with their fluted glass shades that produce a soft luminance over the Pullman bunks where one finds some rare reprints from the N. A. Patterson collection of past great days of life on the rivers; pictures of ships, ports, picnics, skiffs or just fun events.

Each room has its own heater/air conditioning unit with its own controls. The shower room also houses the toilet, which is of the marine type that works on a vacuum system and very little water. Beside the vanity hangs a hair dryer that is always ready to use.

One of the main things in each stateroom is the compact closet that completes the room. As an extra margin of comfort, each stateroom has a separate smoke and heat detector in the ceiling. Also, beside the air conditioner, one will find a 2.5 lb dry chemical fire extinguisher even though the law does not require one in the rooms.

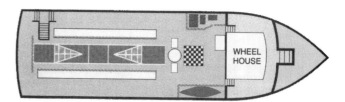

Sun Deck

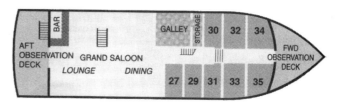

Ottawa Deck

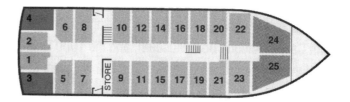

St. Lawrence Deck

Deck map of the three passenger decks

SOME AREAS OF THE SHIP THAT MOST PEOPLE DON'T SEE

THE CREW QUARTERS

The crew quarters is the most forward of the easily accessed non-passenger areas of the ship. It is also the most active area on the ship and is below the St. Lawrence deck. Within this area live the ship's hotel crew and the two deckhands. One of the deck crew is always on duty for everyone's safety. Their job includes the many things that have to be done after hours—cleaning the ship inside and making it ready for the next day.

In all, there are four rooms within this area now. They are all finished with the same bulkhead system that was used in the rest of the ship's construction—doors and all—with the same brass hardware. Each crew room has features like a stateroom, bunks, showers, toilets, sinks, heaters, lockers and air conditioners, but in a more compact layout.

The one difference for the crew is that their port holes on each side of the ship have been fixed closed due to their being so close to the waterline. So each of the four rooms has a separate fresh outside air supply duct with controllable fan.

When the ship was first built, the present female crew room was split into two separate rooms. Since then, the joining wall was removed to create the now larger area, which allows the ladies to enjoy the two complete washrooms. The area now contains six bunks so that crew mixes can contain up to six females if required.

The male crew room, complete with its own washroom, sleeps four when required. The other sleeper room, complete with its own washroom, accommodates two and is a bit larger in area. In most cases we see the ship's purser and the chef enjoy this room.

The sleeper rooms are designed for sleeping only with little room for any thing else. A large part of their area is taken up with the different tanks so the bunks in most cases just fit on the tank tops. These tanks are the fuel and water (potable and gray) tanks of the vessel.

The ship's designer worked very hard creating the living spaces. Though small, they are far larger than the law that is many years old, requires. These three sleeper rooms all enter into the common room at the bottom of the stairs.

The common room area contains a built-in table and seating area, which is the centre for meals and entertainment. To the port side is an area referred to as the tank top.

This carpeted tank top area is the main relaxation section for the off-duty crew holding the TV and VCR. Here the crew can spread out and not be in someone else's way, what with all the crew who keep coming and going due to their different work schedules. The common area also has a separate air conditioning unit for comfort.

Just inside the sliding door of the female room is the escape ladder up to the hatch in the St. Lawrence Deck. As well, there is another fire station.

THE ENGINE ROOM

Aft of the crew quarters is the engine room. It is reached through the forward door of the two doors under the main stairwell that leads up to the Grand Saloon.

This passageway leads down a ladder to the engine room which to most sailors of the world is the heart of the ship. It houses the engines, the pumps, the main electric control panels and transformers plus all the fun items that the engineers love to stroke and polish and write reports about.

Outboard the engine room area are the fuel, holding and fresh water tanks. You enter the engine room port side at the aft bulkhead. Just forward on each side outboard are box-like structures called sea chests. The bottom of the sea chests are the outside hull and are filled with holes. The exhaust system of the main drive engines discharge into the water filled sea chests and is forced out under the hull for a quiet sound. Over top of these chests are the grills with the automatic heat fuse closures that allow the inflow of fresh air for the engine.

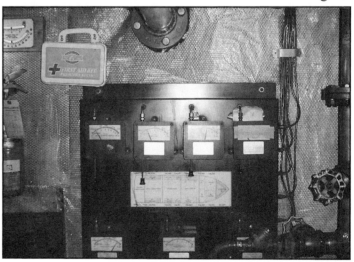

Tank gauges

The two main drives are 365-horse power at 1800 rpm, Volvo light-duty diesel commercial engines These engines turn shafts that are 22 feet long, and extend through the bulkhead into the shaft compartment.

find how much liquid is in each tank. With this help he is better able to keep the ship on an even keel and trim. The cooks have a poor sense of humour when their cakes come out of the ovens wedge shaped.

Just forward of the main engines are a pair of the same type engines driving the generators that put out 135 KW 3-phase electricity, with a 10% overload rating. These two engines exhaust up through the ship, to the stack where sound reducing mufflers are hidden. On the front of each generator engine is a hydraulic pump that drives the bow thruster that is controlled by joysticks in the bridge and one on each of the ship's bridge wings.

Starboard generator with hydraulic pump

In the centre, between the two auxiliary engines that drive the generator/hydraulic pump system, is the chiller unit. This is the heart of the air conditioning system for the whole ship. The top surface is used for a workbench area and is also the engine room library location which contains the manuals for the equipment of the ship and the engine room log book.

Beside the four engines, against the tanks are the banks of batteries to start them. Above the batteries are mounted a cluster of gauges, that contain little hand pumps. These allow the chief to pump up a gauge, to

Just forward, backing against the forward bulkhead, is the switching gear that controls the ship's electrical supply system plus on the port side is the transformer of the electrical system. To the starboard side is the control system for the bow thruster hydraulic system.

Back between the main drive engines are the manifolds, the controlling valves, plus the different pumps that move the liquids between the different tanks including the main fire pumps that feed the fire fighting system of the whole ship. Even though the four engines may be started and controlled from the bridge they still require the loving touch of the engineer to keep them healthy and to operate the minor equipment of the room. The engine room enjoys two escape hatches. One is a standard man hatch, the other is a large rectangle that would allow an engine or generator to be removed through it. They open into the St. Lawrence Deck companionway.

Just forward of the large engine hatch, on the deckhead, is the safety light. The engine room, due to the ever-present possibility of a fire, is protected via a halon firefighting system that is fed from storage tanks in the shaft compartment. This equipment may be released via the bridge or from other control points. For the safety of the crew who may be in the engine room at such a time of need, the light would flash, to give a warning to leave before the gas is discharged to fill the room and smother the fire.

SHAFT COMPARTMENT

Aft of the engine room is the shaft compartment. It is reached through the aft door of the two doors under the main stairwell that leads down a set of stairs. First, the compartment gets it name from the fact the propeller shafts run through this compartment from the engine room through the stuffing boxes to the outside of the ship.

As one proceeds down the set of stairs, one soon learns this is a multipurpose area. It could be called the storage bin or room of the ship but it serves many other needs as well. Under the stairs is a sewage lift station. Here the waste water from the aft part of the ship is pumped into the different holding tanks of the ship to balance the fresh water used from the fresh water tanks.

Under the stairs is the hand-operated bilge pump as part of the safety back-up system. At the bottom of the stair we find the crew's best friend, a clothes washer

and dryer.

Sewage pumping station

Across from the washer and dryer is a lockup for the purser for all of the items of the Corner Store.

Just past the washer and dryer, on the forward bulkhead, you will find the engine room fire extinguisher halon system. Of the four large red cylinders, two are connected to the automatic discharge system and two are for the manual back-up system.

Halon fire fighting system

Above here is the escape hatch from this area. During turn-around time this is the main way to load stores down onto the many shelves.

Next we see the hot water tank system, which supplies the whole ship with hot water. The rest of this area is shelved to hold a wide array of ship's goods. There is a separate area for the different goods, which vary from consumable supplies, spare parts for the many different pieces of equipment aboard the ship, plus a spare parts section for machinery components in the engine room. The range of goods in the shaft compartment at any one time covers the gambit from table napkins and light bulbs to oil filters. The shelving also holds the required linen and towels used for the trip, plus spares.

Between the main hull frames, under the removable wooden floor sections, is the storage area for the dunnage material that could be used to stop up or repair an area in the event of the ship being holed.

TILLER FLATS

The last aft compartment of the ship is what is referred to as the tiller flats.

The flats are reached through a manhole cover in the St. Lawrence Deck companionway just outside of stateroom 5.

The tiller flats are where the hydraulic rudder controls are located to turn the twin balanced rudders. Here you would find stored the equipment ready to connect to the steering gear in an emergency to provide a backup control in the event the ship lost its steering connection from the bridge. Crew members would be directed via a telephone to the bridge. With the two separately controlled systems for each engine, which turn separate drive shafts and props, the captain would have full steering control if required.

The flats are also a major storage place for containers of new and used oils, plus any oily bilge water as such, waiting to be offloaded ashore, or for any other materials that are not required every day or not very often.

UNDERWAY
AT
LAST

THE FIRST TRIPS

The first passenger trip from Kingston departed Sept. 27, 1981. It was down the river to Upper Canada Village and back. A three-nighter with layovers at Alexandria Bay, Upper Canada Village, and Gananoque.

The wheelhouse interior was not finished, nor were the crew quarters even built then. All the crew had to sleep in staterooms till we would get their quarters finished.

Three of us, fitter/shipwrights and carpenters, sailed onboard and worked whenever we could. The problem was not to disturb the passengers and their trip. It was also a problem of not interfering with the operation and/or navigation of the ship and to get the ship finished inside. Have you ever been involved with a stage producer who wants the set changed without distracting the players who are performing in center stage? Need-less to say we had fun.

It was a very historical trip for all on board. Ship whistles sounded the whole trip whenever another vessel came within range. It was difficult to saw and work in the bridge as the radio chatter never stopped. Everyone wanted to see the ship and talk with the captain, Chris McCarney. He was well liked throughout the islands.

The next trip was the most famous of all trips in many ways. It was the first trip to Ottawa up the Rideau Canal system that the ship was designed and built for.

Passengers and a lot of media including a TV crew, boarded September 30, 1981 in the early evening.

Those aboard, including special guests for the evening, enjoyed a cruise of the harbor and the city lights before tying up at the La Salle Causeway North Wall to overnight in Kingston's inner harbour. This was the plan due to the Causeway Bridge being closed to shipping during morning rush hours.

The ship would have been delayed for over two hours in the morning had it stayed at the Brock St. dock overnight, due to road traffic over the causeway.

Marine traffic, due to the low volume, took second place to the needs of motor vehicle operators wanting to get to work on time. They were not interested in the marine history that was being made as they rushed to work that day.

The ship departed on time at 7:00 a.m. Oct.1, 1981 and made history that soon was on the front pages of all the nation's media. The ship got more free ink than planned for. Much more than anyone had dreamed of.

The January press release of the construction of the ship only just whetted the media's appetite compared to what lay ahead.

We had worked flat out for over three weeks without a break to get the ship operational, burning the candle at both ends, as they say.

So, after the first trip down to Upper Canada Village and back, Bob Clark suggested I take the night off and visit my home and family since I lived in Kingston at that time. What a feeling to have a hot bath and to sleep in my own bed!

The suggested plan was for me to rejoin the ship at Kingston Mills, which is just north east of the city, sometime after eight the next morning. The idea was that I could sleep in. The ship would be some time going through the locks of Kingston Mills.

My son, Shawn, skipped school and came along with his mother and I for the history lesson that morning. We, and others in the know, stopped and stood on the 401 bridge over the Cataraqui River that the ship would have to pass under. Soon others stopped and asked what was up, for we had no fish poles. What was in the water that we were looking for, and all kinds of questions. We told them of the *Canadian Empress* coming upriver for the first time.

The Kingston Mills Locks were just upriver. We watched with great joy for this was to be the first ship of any size or its type in many, many years that was going to be navigating this great river/canal system.

The *Canadian Empress* came into sight. People, who had stopped, joined us in cheering. What a sight! It was the first time I had seen the ship moving underway. It was like something one would see in a movie of Tom Sawyer. The *Canadian Empress* came up the channel, the crew lowered its stack and masts for this first bridge of the trip.

Strange things were happening that many people

never noticed and fewer understood. The ship was causing bank and bottom suction.

Even though she was traveling at a slow speed, the shallow river bottom sucked the ship down, which in turn was setting a wake wash to run along the shore.

The 401 bridge

This was to be a big event for the TV and other media crew aboard to watch and document. Some crews were to be set up on the shore and lock walls to capture the history of the ship traveling upbound through the lock system it had been designed to navigate.

Captain Chris McCarney slowed the vessel to a crawl and with a blast of its horn to the people on the bridge, it passed below, everyone on deck looking to see how much clearance she had. Yes, horn is the right word for we had not yet obtain the blessing of an air powered whistle system and we did not have steam to blow the whistle.

Under the bridge with safe passage she went. Like little kids we shouted and waved, cheered and cried, at the same time as we ran to the other side to watch it move upstream.

Those on board the top deck ran to the stern and returned our waves and shouts as the *Canadian Empress* traveled around the bend in the river and out of sight.

Again like a bunch of school kids we raced back across the road. Quickly we hopped in our cars and raced by road around to where the ship would dock at the sea wall of the canal below the first lock.

Remember the *Canadian Empress's* size, 4 feet 9 inches in depth, a beam of 30 feet and a length of 108 feet. Would it fit? Would it fit easily? It had passed the height test under the first bridge of the system that it met when it sailed under the 401. Would the wooden timber fenders hanging on the side have to be lifted out of the way to give clearance? A lot of questions floated in my mind and others.

Now Came The Fit-in-the-box Test

All these questions had been asked many, many times in the past, especially in the last few hours by those who sat onboard the night before. Now was the time for the real hard facts to surface of the Rideau Canal system and the *Canadian Empress*.

Would They Match?

What a surprise. It was hard to think of what really was taking place. We never realized that we were a part of this new history. We had parked the car at the upper lock and were walking down the path to the lower lock.

Me—I had my satchel in hand as it was a workday once all this locking fun was over with. People were everywhere. Everyone was taking pictures. As we rounded the turning basin between locks 46 and 47, we turned to go down the lock stairs where I planned to shoot some photos as the ship slipped into the lower lock.

Big Surprise Time

The lower lock gate was not open yet and the **Canadian Empress** was tied up alongside. Most of all was the surprise to find the passengers were filing along the path coming up towards us with no smiles on their faces. What was really strange and then shocking of this caterpillar line was to see them with their life jackets on.

The dock at Kigston Mills Lock

At first the vision did not relate, for it was a funny place or time to hold the required fire drill that must be held within twenty four hours of leaving a port with a load of new passengers. They did, though, look very colourful with their bright orange life vests against the backdrop of fall colour and granite rocks of the area.

I quickly learned it was no drill nor a chance for them all to stand around the lock and watch the ship enter the first lock as many had planned to do.

Big trouble, was the words were heard. The ship had made contact with an unknown rock in midchannel just North of the 401 bridge about a mile from the first lock. This was just after the bend in the river, where we last saw her.

The captain, Chris McCarney, did not wish to lose his ship. He knew, just ahead were the docks, at the foot of the lock.

The boat and fire drill were for real as the cold river water was flooding into the ship. It was fall and the trees were in full splendor, as he sounded the alarm.

SOS...SOS...SOS,

With the calm of his vast experience, the ship was safely put alongside for the passengers to get ashore.

In a moment the shock of reality can stun the mind. Thousands of pictures flood the brain, your senses awash with emotions. Perception is reality. The people are leaving the ship. The crew are doing their jobs.

CHAPTER TWENTY-SIX   Building the LAST CANADIAN CRUISE SHIP

The Damn Ship Is Sinking!

Like bloody hell!. Pride, stupidity, or that gut need to answer a call for help, one just does things at times and later tries to understand the whys. To hell with Murphy and his Law. He was not going to steal my boat, my blood, my sweat and tears and that of all the others. That damn ship was not sinking if we had our way.

At first the deck crew would not let us board. They had their orders and their training was really being tested. They were told to just get everyone safely off. At that time, saving people was more important than saving the ship. The engineer and other workers who had boarded in Kingston were inspecting the hull in every compartment.

But there was more than one way to board the ship, so we just bypassed them. They were busy at the side embarkation. Back to the bow, over the rail and up the forward stairs heading to the bridge, I and some other late-arriving workers went.

The captain was pleased to see us for he understood we had knowledge and skills from having just built the ship that could assist him deeply.

Down to the crew quarters, I was directed. It was a good thing the crew quarters were not finished for that was where the hole was punched in the ship.

"Get the floor up fast. Water's coming in there."

"Tell the chief I will need shoring and a runner for tools and material"

"Done. I will send help down"

The engineer was pumping tanks and lightening the ship where possible, as fast as he could.

Crew quarters, yea, sure. I could see water in the stair well even before opening the fire door at the bottom of the stairwell. The area was more then wet. Water was everwhere, but so were the tools we had left there yesterday when we last worked here. Some were already under a foot of water. Before the plates were removed the compartment would be flooded three foot deep.

It is was a very waking feeling as your hands and legs went numb.

Again, pride, stupidity or just plain stubbornness, whatever the reason, we blocked out the pain and found unknown reserve and stayed on the job at hand.

Remember Kim, the young lady from the engine room? Well she was now an offical deckhand, working on her first marine emergency, right beside me in the icy water as we both joked about our numb bums and toes that did not feel like they were there any more. Idle chatter helped to overcome the pain and fear the rising cold water was causing.

"How High The Water Momma? I'm Not Tel'n."

I had learned years before as a volunteer fire captain that foolish chatter was at times a safe way to work with others in very dangerous situations. The chit chat took your mind off the danger around you. That voice of someone else in the same danger gave comfort that you were not alone, that we would make it.

In the back of my mind was... a sinking...at any minute. This was no simple job. The lock may only be 5 feet 6 inches deep but the channel at the dock was at least 15 feet. All those stories read of ships going down! The vison of the **Canadian Empress** with water awash in the Grand Saloon was not grand in my mind. My grandmother and her sinking, flashed into my mind. But she had wind, rain, and waves plus the cold dark of a November night. Plus she did not have the pumps we had to help stop the flow of water.

At least it was not dark. But power was a problem. The chief engineer shut down power to the crew quarters for everyone's safety.

Everything we did was hand labour. Even using two foot long screw drivers was a problem. It was hard to hold them in the screw slots but at last with our heads under water sometimes as we worked bent over, searching and working more screws out of their holes. At last we were able to unbolt the crew floor decking and expose the ruptured hull plates. Now the water really came in. We blocked the fear as others passed us dunnage and shoring to brace the padding in place. One thing about the cold water of the river—it was clear and clean, so we could see what we were doing.

Once the dunnage was shored in place it retarded the inflow of water. Now we were able to control the situation with the ship's pumps to keep her afloat. Soon extra pumps from the local fire department arrived. They really saved the day and gave us a rest and a bigger comfort zone.

News traveled fast. We found out later we were reported to be sinking out in the St. Lawrence River and then it was Lake Ontario. So much for the media that was right there at first hand.

A New Problem Arose

There were no drydocks within safe navigation range that could haul the ship. They were in use with other ships being repaired or inspected. It was wait for several weeks, or a long trip on Lake Ontario for a wounded ship that was not designed for such a trip and at a time of year for storms on the lake. Neither one was an enjoyable factor for the owner or the insurance company officials.

Soon a plan was hatched to use the second lock as a drydock. Due to its height above the lower lock flood level, it could easily be drained and used as a drydock.

Being late in season helped, because there were only a few other vessels in the system. They required clearing before the ship could be drydocked.

At last the ship got to test the locks for size. All went well as the vessels made good passage through and into lock two. All went well as lock two drained and the ship settled onto the bed of cribbing that had been placed on the lock's floor.

Ten days after the sickening blow to the hull, the ship was repaired, and sailed, without passengers, up the remaining locks at Kingston Mills, then to the first buoy north of the locks. Here, the captain sounded the ship's horn. He came about and returned to Kingston to finish the fall season on the St. Lawrence.

Out of all the bad came some good as it gave us some time to finish the bridge as the repairs were made to the ship's hull by other workers.

It took Bob and the lawyers eight years to win the court case against the government. The government knew of the rock, its location and its problem to navigation as many others had hit it before, yet they had failed to remove it or expose its true nature to canal users.

As they say in the courts of law, with a term I find disgusting "The government was less than honest."

Captain Chris McCarney has a chunk of the rock, taken from the hull rip, as a pendent, on a chain around his neck to remember that day. Bob Clark, the owner has a section of the hull plate with the slashing cut from that rock.

Hard Facts,
Murphy's Law Can And Did Make History

The charts reported the channel had a clearance of 5 feet 6 inches at datum, which in true life at contact time was closer to 7 feet of water depth due to the high water level. The top of the rock, which had been reported as being struck by many other vessels, including the local provincial police patrol boat, was found at about depth of 3 feet in centre channel. It was not a small stone. It was proven that Parks Canada knew of it being there but failed to report, publish or remove it. The ship drew 4 feet 9 inches and as they say, the rest is history because the ship has never made another attempt to go to Ottawa via the Rideau Canal system. A true shame. It has been reported that they changed the charts and rules for ships wishing to navigate the system.

Over the winter many little details were completed aboard the ship.

Spring Of 82

The first trip to Montréal was spring of 82. Then we went on to Québec City.

After disembarking the passengers in Québec City, it was time for more special public relations—a harbour cruise and dinner for different people from different government departments including Tourism and Liquor License Board officials.. The ship required a license to sell liquor while the vessel was in Québec waters.

The powers to be were impressed with the ship and her standards of service. The much-needed license was awarded.

The next day the ship opened its gangways to the passengers of the *New Shorm* that just happened to tie up astern of the **Canadian Empress**. What a surprise they found! But they were soon disappointed. They would have to book another time as we were off to Three Rivers before going to Montréal for more public relations stops. At Three Rivers the boarding lineup was over a half-mile long. Word had traveled fast from our stop there two days before.

The **Canadian Empress** is only one of a few ships that can legally have the bar open at the dock or underway in both Upper and Lower Canada.

SOME CHANGES OVER THE YEARS

Present day logo

Since the *Canadian Empress* was completed there have been some changes to different areas of the ship.

The *Canadian Empress* started out as the first vessel of the Rideau - St. Lawrence Cruise Ships. After that time when it was decided not to run the Rideau Canal system, the firm changed its corporate name to St. Lawrence Cruise Lines Inc.

Each year critique lists are made from all the comment cards the passenger and crew fill in after each trip. These are reviewed to determine what, if any, repairs or changes are required that would make life on board more enjoyable to all.

Also, there are the detailed yearly 'look and see' inspections of this twenty-year-old lady. Commencing with the winter layup work, the inspections continue over the fall and winter every year. Some are simple and others are involved.

The good lord made us all different, but the bunks on the ship are all the same length. So an answer was found for those tall people who love to criuse. In a few of the staterooms for different reasons, it was found that a mattress extender could be fitted, so these were custom made for these special bunks. Now the tall passengers can enjoy a full-length sleep.

One of the main areas of change that a passenger would not really notice but use all the time, are the wooden handrails around the outside of the ship. No matter what we do to preserve or restore their finish, Mother Nature gets to do her thing to the western hemlock of the railings.

Each fall they are removed and inspected for breaks or damage, before being stored for the winter inside. Come spring the restored or replaced rails are once again refitted. Even with this work, the railings have all been replaced at least twice over the ship's lifetime.

Along the length of the ship are two rub rails. When the ship was first built they were made of oak with their matching adjustable oak fenders. The oak rub rails took a hard beating in the different locks so they were replaced with a black neoprene that has stood up very well under the strain they get on some windy days.

It was soon found that the different levels of docks and sea walls of the locks and the ever-changing level of the rivers required more embarkation gates to the different level of decks to avoid the steep and some times impossible gangway slopes.

Another change enjoyed by all indirectly, but mainly by the ship's captains directly, was the addition of GPI (Global Position Indicator) navigation equipment on the bridge. For the few times a year that Mother Nature reduces the visibility, the captain can use GPI, as an extra pair of eyes in addition to the radar. There are those places on the rivers where the compass can take on a mind of it own due to the magnetic fields like the one in Kingston's Harbor. It is not a nice feeling to watch a compass spin like a top when the ship is travelling in a straight line.

Time found that people enjoy the bow area to view where the ship is headed. To make this passtime more enjoyable, requests were made asking for the creation of a shaded resting area. The fore deck was covered over with a traditional canvas awning of yellow with a yellow and white skirt, supported by a white pipe framework. This arrangement provides a shade and rain cover that all have enjoyed yearly.

At different times of the year on the rivers one gets to enjoy the many happenings of Mother Nature. May and June are a fisherman's joy as the Mayflies, for a few days, make their metamorphic pop out of the water as they make their change from a larva in water to flying around in great masses; a great food supply and treat for all those fish the fishermen are trying to catch! For all aboard the vessel, it is an annual event to see but not have close contact with. They cause no real harm, just the mess to clean each day as they die after a short life. At the same time another piece of nature that is not so loved by man, woman or beast is our famous Canadian mosquito. For others it is the black flies.

A way was found to assist the passengers in a quest to fully enjoy Mother Nature's yearly happenings and the great views of the ever-changing river but not at such close contact these events can give us.

One of the problems to be overcome was that every time the ship arrived or departed a dock, the deck crew had to handle the lines that ran ashore. Creative thinking and Velcro® now gives the ship a screened stern deck complete with a heritage style screen door in the stairwell to the top deck. Zip! They're on! Zip! They're off! The screens just roll up for storage when not required.

When the ship was first built, smoking was an acceptable thing. Time and laws change so the *Canadian Empress* was made a smoke-free vessel. When built, there had been the large electronic air filter that hung over the Grand Saloon stairwell. It was removed and replaced with an antique brass lamp that matches the wall sconces of the room. The air filter unit still has a life in a marine setting. Last seen it was in the bar at The Thousand Island Marina east of Kingston.

The soft lighting of the Grand Saloon in the evening is a crowning touch to a great day on the water—just to sit around and relax. For some of the different enterrainment the lighting lacked a lot. It did not always provide suitable lighting, so a small section of track lighting was fitted to brighten up the show areas as needed.

The tin plate ceilings (deckheads) of the ship create a nostalgic feeling of being on an old river steamship. This image was further enhanced with some regulation changes in 1993. With these changes the *Canadian Empress* was allowed more exposed wooden surfaces on the outside of the ship. Nineteen Ninety-four, found me creating and installing the red cedar planking with oiled finish and hundreds of brass screws, on the deckhead, and on the aft deck bulkhead complete with the oak toerail to take the everyday wear.

Included are hidden hatches to get to important things that require service from time to time. The same treatment with the red cedar also dresses the brow of the foredeck and deckhead under the captain's walk.

Funny, everyone wants sunny holidays and then complains how hot it is when the sun is out. Big sun umbrellas were fitted to the top deck for shade for that after-lunch nap or leisure viewing.

For the many who suffer bad hair days we installed hair blowers in every stateroom. Another room change was the adding of a shoe shelf fitted in the bottom of the closets.

In the winter of 1996-7, I created a complete new bar/liquor display cabinet, which allowed an even larger display of liquors. The roll away tambours took less space to store than the old locking door panels that were a problem every day.

Again we replaced the wooden railings topside. Another change that most would never see but enjoy was the replacement of all the Grand Saloon windows with thermo-pain windows units. Now they don't have the problem of window's fogging up.

The curtains of the Grand Saloon have also been replaced. When built they were of burgundy velvet. The strong sun through the glass windows rotted them so now one sees deep green velvet curtains.

There was talk, for several years, of wooden handrails for the bow deck. This turned into another long-time dream come true. It took two years just to find clear hemlock of a size needed to make the rails. Their installation brought joy to many.

In 2001 the companionways of the ship got a major upgrade. In the past the decks had been re-laid with vinyl tiles at different times. But they always wore badly as companionways are high and heavy traffic sections of the ship. Luggage and ship's stores at time snagged the edges of the tiles. A flooring material was found that gave the ship a planked floor look. The team who installed it did a great job.

What's funny is that as the ship gets older, it looks better, and more in keeping with its intended concept. Many of the passengers who return each year are faced with the puzzling test to discover what are the newest events in the constant changes and upgrades to "their" ship. Some think of the ship that way as they have crusied many years aboard.

One of the latest changes they will find is the addition to the vessel of a new small Charlie Noble to exhaust the heat from the Ottawa Deck companionway caused by the ice cube machine. The first machine was water cooled. The new one is air cooled. It works better with less noise and other problems.

For some it was spotting the new sign "skirts" on the side of the gangway that the passengers can see and use many times during a voyage,

In 2003 came the completion of the new digital sound system for the ship. This helped improve the sound of all things, from the speakers on the ship and including a new location for the Grand Saloon entertainment system.

NOTHING
IS IMPOSSIBLE

THE GOOD DREAMER

As you have read, the ***M/V Canadian Empress*** was the result of some fanciful thinking on the part of Bob Clark in 1979.

Having been actively involved in architecture, real estate and the housing industry, Bob's entrepreneurial spirit wouldn't allow him to let go of this idea and within a very short period of time the keel for the ship was being laid. The ***M/V Canadian Empress*** was launched on September 5/6th, 1981.

He had chosen the year 1908 as a design and decor theme because Bob wanted a vessel that would

Robert W. 'Bob' Clark

integrate well with the history of the St. Lawrence River. The ***M/V Canadian Empress*** is not a replica of any specific vessel, but is a composite replica of many vessels that were common in the St. Lawrence region during the turn-of-the-last century.

Over the years, the ***M/V Canadian Empress*** has been host to guests from virtually every province of Canada, every state in the United States and numerous countries throughout the world.

In 1990, St. Lawrence Cruise Lines Inc. was named Business of the Year by the Greater Kingston,

Ontario, Chamber of Commerce, and in 1997, Bob Clark was named Business Person of the Year by the chamber.

Another honour was again bestowed in 2003—Business Person of the Year by the Kingston Whig Standard (a local newspaper) as Bob had acquired ownership of a 55-year-old landmark resturant in Kingston known as Aunt Lucy's and set about restoring it to a dinner house. The story of both of our involvements past and present in this eatery is another story for another time.

As we who know Bob say, "When he Clarkifies it, it will be great again."

Bob is a firm believer in a 'hands-on' management style, always looking for improvements. It's not uncommon to find Bob and his wife Mryna cruising on board with passengers—taking just a little time from work to enjoy the scenic beauty of these wonderful rivers that they have shared with many in the world.

He's even been known to buy you a drink on board the *Canadain Empress* or a butterscotch Sunday at Aunt Lucy's.

THIS DREAMER

Executive Officer Mate Preston (1982)

I too have been a dreamer at times as well, like all dreamers do about something. One was to someday write a book.

Well, what started as notes for a speaking engagement in 2001 for the Learning and Leisure Group of Peterborough, Ontario turned into the storyboard that created this book as I milked my mind and sweet memories, sorting, confirming fact, and fiction.

It was a labour of love for something that has been a real perception for a quarter century. I thank those that heard of my dream and wanted to share their memories. So you have read and have proof that some dreams come true, and this dream is now a book.

As I clear up and store all the papers, notes and pictures that created this book I find a new storyboard by collecting tales and memories that are and were a part of the **Canadian Empress** dreams and histories.

They are simple stories of people like you. There is one of a lady who found that 'Player pianos don't lie', another one of 'a lady who cried when a officer joined her for dinner'.

We even have the mystery of 'the passenger who jumped ship in mid voyage'. The question is, why? The how and why he was aboard is fact.

'Why would people fly 3000 miles from the English Islands for a corn roast?' Yes, they did and it is most interesting. 'The honeymooners that did not have gray hair.'

As you see many interesting things have happen aboard my girl since I first fell in love with her.
I trust the grand lady, the **Canadian Empress** is a joy in your heart too.

The man on the left is the master builder René Longtin
the man who operated the Algan Boat Yard
that gave birth to these dreams
This moment in time was captured
during the shakedown cruise spring 2002
The other builder is me
There is more to this picture then meets the eye
but that is for the next book

Me feeding the ducks at Upper Canada Village 1982

So send your sweet memories for consideration and possible addition to my storyboard, in my dream-land, in care of :-

Robbie Preston
171 Rink St. Suite 278
Peterborough, Ontario
K9J 2J6

If you send a picture or three make sure you sign the back with an open release so that we can freely use them.

The Good Lord willing, we may share more.

GLOSSORY

NAUTICAL TERMS	LAND LUBBER TERMS
Ballast Tanks	Storage tanks on the ship that may be filled with non-potable water.
Beam	The width of the ship.
Bow	The pointed end of the ship. The front or forward end of a vessel.
Bow Thruster	A transverse propeller mounted in a tube in the bow of the ship, used to push the bow of the vessel sideways.
Bridge	Also called the wheelhouse, the area of the vessel from where the captain controls the ship.
Bridge Wings	The area of the control stations outside the bridge at the side of the ship.
Bulkhead	A wall-like construction inside a ship.
Bumpers	Rubber, plastic or inflatable tube-shape fenders that hang over the side of the ship for protection.
Carling Floats	Red flat floating life rafts.
Compartments	The rooms of a ship below the main deck.
Companionways	The hallways of a ship.

Charlie Noble	A rotatable air vent, also called mushroom vent or funnel
Chiller	The main unit of an air conditioning supply system.
Chine	A sharp line edge of where the hull plates meet and change angles.
Combing	Raised pieces of bulkhead around openings in a deck,
Corner Store	Gift or tuck shop of a ship.
D of T	A Doctor of Tinkering. An expert or master of many fields of work. One who is overly creative and/or a problem solver.
Draft	How much water the ship needs to float. Canadian Empress draft is 4 feet 9 inches.
Draws	The depth a vessel projecting down into the water, also called draft.
Dunnage	Padding and lumber braces used to stop the flow of water (see shoring)
Drum-taut	As in the ropes were under tention enough that one could walk on them without sag.
Embarkation	A point of entry to a vessel.
Forepeak	A storage compartment or area in the bow of a ship. Usually paint and rope is stored there.
Fenders	The wooden rub rails that hang on the side of the ship, (see bumpers).
Freeboard	The amount of height on the side of the vessel above the water.
Galley	Ship's kitchen.
Holding Tanks	Sewage tanks.
Hull	The frame or body of a ship.
Inflatables	Self-inflating life rafts. One just pulls the painter out of the container to open them.
Joystick	Control lever for the bow thruster.
Knot	An interlacing of rope, cord, etc, drawn tight into a lump or end.

	A measure of Nautical speed about 1.125 statute miles per hour.
L. O. A.	Length overall of a vessel.
Log	This is the official record log book of the ship's happenings.
	There is also an official engine room log book.
	A device for measuring the speed of a ship.
Master	The captain of a merchant ship.
Mate	An officer of a merchant vessel ranking below the captain.
Murphy's Law	"If anything can go wrong, it will" was first cited at Edwards Air Force Base in 1949 by Captain Edward Murphy.
Nigger's Nest	An old sailing term for the area of the vessel that the crew lives in.
Painter	A rope fastened to an inflatable life raft to secure it to the vessel.
	Also it is the means to open the life raft.

Port	A place on land with a dock that a ship can tie up to.
Port side	Looking forward, it is the left side of the ship.
Potable	Fit to drink
Purser's Office	Purser's hideaway, where all of the ship business is conducted
Radio	Ship-to-ship or ship-to-shore radio communication equipment on the Bridge.
Rope pudding	A bumper or fender made of a rope core with a braided rope covering.
Salamander	A big electric barbeque used in the galley to cook food.
Saloon	A large room or hall for receptions, public entertainment, or exhibitions. A large social lounge on a passenger ship. A place where alcoholic drinks are sold and drunk..
Scrambled eggs	fancy gold scroll work on a officer's hat brim.
Shaft	A metal rod of large diameter

that connects the engine to the prop.

Shaft Compartment The ship's storeroom. Also a place on a vessel where the drive shafts penetrate the hull.

Starboard Looking forward it is the right side of the vessel.

Ship A vessel that carries a boat.

Shipwright A carpenter who specializes in carpentry and joinery work for a ship.

Ship's Telegraph A pedestal in the bridge that contains levers and indicators to convey and show bridge signals to the engine room and back. Not used on the *Canadian Empress* but one is there for show.

Shore stores The supply room where all general stores are kept untill required.

Shoring Wood bracing used to keep the dunnage in place over a damaged area of a vessel. (see dunnage)

Springline A line from the ship, tied forward or aft to stop the ship from surg-

ing when at the dock.

Stern The very back end of a vessel.

Strong backs Longitudinal beams built into the upper-most deck to provide extra stiffness to the hull to reduce sagging.

Thruster See bow thruster.

Tumble Home The inward sloping of the ship sides from the vertical. Note: None on the *Canadian Empress*.

Watch The length of shift time a crew member works at one time.

Ways A place where vessels are built with sloping ways down to the water.

Wheelhouse The section of the Bridge where the ship's steering wheel is located .

ILLUSTRATIONS AND PHOTOGRAPHS

ILLUSTRATIONS

On the cover and throughout the book one will find the etching of the ship sitting in a tranquil cove. In studying the etching one can see an image of the model (page 26). The artist B. Droppo used photographs of the scale model to create this famous image. The image was used by the company on their first brochure to promote sales before the ship was completed.

PHOTOGRAPHS

For Illustration and photographs on page 8, 21, (2 on) 30, (2 on) 31, 32, 37, 38, (2 on) 39, 40, 44, 109, 110, 115, 121. Plus the Etching of the ship used on the cover and throughout the book we wish to thank Bob and Myrna Clark and St. Lawrence Cruise Lines Inc. for the generous contribution of photographs from their collection.

Illustration and photographs on page 2, 9, 19, (2 on) 22, 26, 62, 63. (2 on) 64, 67, 68, 69, 71, 72, 75, (2 on) 76, 77, 78, (2 on) 79, (2 on) 80, 81, 82, 83, 84, 85, 86, 87, (3 on) 88, 89, (2 on) 90, 97, 98, 101,102, 123, (2 on) 124, are from the author's collection.

All photographs used in this publication are copyrights of the photographer/owner.

To order more copies of

Building the **LAST CANADIAN CRUISE SHIP**

by
Robert W. Preston

send

$24.95

plus $9.00
GST, Postage and Handling

to

*Press
On
Endeavors*

171 Rink St. Suite 278, Peterborough, Ontario, Canada, K9J 2J6

Telephone 705-876-9571

press_on@mac.com